Modern
Fiesta
1986-Present

Schiffer Publishing Ltd
380 Lower Valley Road, Atglen, PA 19310 USA

Terri Polick

Dedication

To the memory of Jonathan O. Parry.

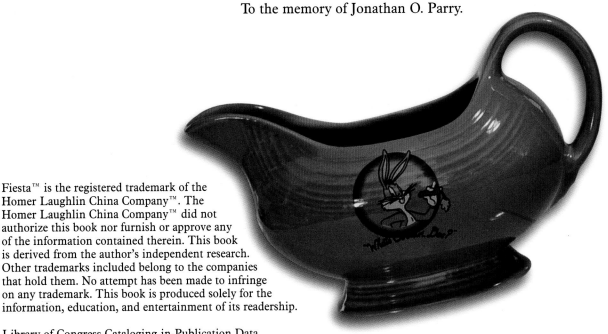

Fiesta™ is the registered trademark of the
Homer Laughlin China Company™. The
Homer Laughlin China Company™ did not
authorize this book nor furnish or approve any
of the information contained therein. This book
is derived from the author's independent research.
Other trademarks included belong to the companies
that hold them. No attempt has been made to infringe
on any trademark. This book is produced solely for the
information, education, and entertainment of its readership.

Library of Congress Cataloging-in-Publication Data

Polick, Terri.
Modern Fiesta, 1986-present / by Terri Polick.
p. cm.
ISBN 0-7643-1702-4
1. Homer Laughlin China Company--Catalogs. 2. Fiesta ware--
Collectors and collecting--Catalogs. 3. Pottery, American--West
Virginia--Newell--20th century--Catalogs. 4. Parry, Jonathan Owen,
1948- 1. Title.
NK421.H65 A4 2003
738'.09754'12075--dc21
2002013321

Back cover: "Orange Fiesta" by Philip J. Carroll. Oil on canvas, 50 inches x
36 inches, collection of the artist. *Courtesy of Philip J. Carroll.*

Designed by Bonnie M. Hensley
Cover design by Bruce M. Waters
Type set in Seagull Hv BT/Aldine721 BT

ISBN: 0-7643-1702-4
Printed in China
1 2 3 4

Published by Schiffer Publishing Ltd.
4880 Lower Valley Road
Atglen, PA 19310
Phone: (610) 593-1777; Fax: (610) 593-2002
E-mail: Schifferbk@aol.com
Please visit our web site catalog at **www.schifferbooks.com**
We are always looking for people to write books on new and
related subjects. If you have an idea for a book please contact
us at the above address.

This book may be purchased from the publisher.
Include $3.95 for shipping.
Please try your bookstore first.
You may write for a free catalog.

In Europe, Schiffer books are distributed by
Bushwood Books
6 Marksbury Ave.
Kew Gardens
Surrey TW9 4JF England
Phone: 44 (0)20-8392-8585
Fax: 44 (0)20-8392-9876
E-mail: Bushwd@aol.com
Free postage in the UK. Europe: air mail at cost

Contents

Acknowledgments

Former First Lady Hillary Clinton said it takes a village to raise a child. I can add that it takes a community of collectors to write a book. It was my heartfelt wish to write a book that not only documented the history of post 86 Fiesta, but honored a great artist, my friend, Jonathan Parry. I wish to thank Jonathan's mother, Dorothy Tims, and his aunt, Gene-Ellen Walton, for providing me with family photographs and interviews for the book. I also want to offer special thanks to Jonathan's son, Parker Parry, and Jonathan's former wife, Carol Parry. Parker allowed me to photograph his father's Fiesta collection and without his support and cooperation many unique pieces, never photographed before, would not have been included in this book. Carol Parry offered her support and friendship. As a talented writer, Carol Parry not only offered me technical assistance in putting this book together but her friendship as well. She offered me personal insights into Jonathan's life and, as a member of the Aaron family, Carol also provided information about her family's role in the reintroduction of Fiesta.

Many Fiesta collectors and dealers also helped me with the book and I hope I don't inadvertently miss anyone's name. Gary Schreiner, Joel Wilson, Kathy Garrels, Ellie Rovella, Nina Morrison, and Harvey Linn deserve special thanks for all their extra effort in helping with the book. Harvey let me come to his house and photograph his collections on one of his rare days off from work. Ellie, Gary, Kathy, and Joel sent me pictures and also allowed me to photograph items from their collections. Kathy and Joel also let me borrow items for the cover shot. Nina did some shopping for me and sent me some dishes not available in my area. They all offered me special words of encouragement and I will never forget their kindness. I would also like to thank Rick Benning, Angie Pickens, and Rick Guizzotti for providing information for the book and Jo Cunningham and Fred Mutchler for offering me moral support on those days when it seemed like everything was going wrong. Most importantly, I want to thank my family for their ongoing help and encouragement. Without their support, this book would not have been possible.

The following people also gave much needed support during the writing of this book.

Deb Ahdoot	Arleen Kennedy	Paul Perkol
Lynette Burnett	Bob Larimer	Steven Prickett
Mark Burnett	Tim Maleck	Jim Russell
Richard Capps	Patrick Masterson	Thomas Sandretto
Philip Carroll	John Mattingly	Don Schreckengost
John Finn	Charles & Dorothy Morrison	Jeryl Schreiner
		Pat Shreve
Terry Fogel	Nina Morrison	Therese Smith
Ralph Franke	Paul Murawski	Joe Solito
Mark Gonzalez	Dennis Newbury	Troy Williams
Charles Hall	Carolyn Olbum	
Lynn Blocker-Krantz		

Finally, I would like to thank Bruce Waters for his hard work on the cover art.

Foreword

I vividly remember the first time I became aware of Fiestaware. I was about five years old and my grandfather, Louis K. Friedman, visited us in Pittsburgh. He went down to "the Pottery," as we all referred to Homer Laughlin, and returned with a set of four Fiesta coffee mugs. I still remember the colors: medium green, yellow, orange, and turquoise. I adored them on sight, and made everyone in the family promise that they were only for me. I used them constantly, at every meal, and broke them one by one until the turquoise was the last one remaining.

When I married Jonathan Parry on July 5, 1974, he already knew about Fiesta. Since childhood he was a avid collector of antique art glass and pottery. I remember discussing Fiesta with him and commenting that they really should bring it back, because everyone obviously still liked it as much as ever. Years later, after he had gone to work at the Pottery, I suggested that

Carol's grandfather, Louis K Friedman. *Photo courtesy of Carol Parry.*

he ask my Uncle Lester (Marcus Aaron II) about it. Each evening when he would come home from work I would ask him, "Did you see Uncle Lester today?", and Jon would reply either yes or no. Then, if the answer was "yes" I would follow up with, "Well, did you ask him about Fiesta?" And Jon would always answer "No." We would both laugh and I would drop the subject until the next day. One day, I went into the usual routine, and the answer to the second question was "Yes." "Well, what did he say?", I countered hopefully. "No," Jon replied, and we both sighed. Still, we were both hopeful that one day it might happen, and Jon began to work on samples of new colors that he thought would be appropriate. He would occasionally bring home a plate in one of these sample colors for us to try out, but it would take a few more years before my cousin, Pete (Marcus Aaron III), would take over the reins at Homer Laughlin and post 86 Fiesta would become a reality.

Jon loved color as much as I do. He insisted on painting the living room a certain shade of pale apricot in every home we ever owned (and we bought and sold four of them during our eleven year marriage). The original Post-86 "Apricot" color is exactly the same as the one he always chose for our living rooms. We didn't always agree about color though. My absolute favorite color is the one that post 86 Fiesta collectors know as "Chartreuse." Even though we had divorced amicably by the time that color came out, he told me that was "my" color. Between us, Jon always called that color "puke green," but I think he did it just to tease me.

That early set of Fiesta mugs left an indelible impression on me. The colors and the blocky-curvy 1940s shapes all remained favorites of mine. Almost a decade ago, under the name of Karima Parry, I went on to start Plastic Fantastic, a website where I deal in Bakelite jewelry, and to write three books about Bakelite jewelry. And I don't find it strange at all that many Bakelite collectors tell me that they also love Fiesta. Both Fiesta and Bakelite jewelry are happy, bright, and sculptural. They are fun to look at and fun to own and use and, for those reasons, I believe they will always remain popular.

We all miss Jon, but I am reminded of him constantly, because post 86 Fiesta is everywhere. Not a day goes by that I don't see it in magazines, on television, and in countless homes and collections around the world. Fiesta has become a beloved American design icon. Post 86 Fiesta brought Fiesta in a whole new palette of colors to a whole new generation who treasures it as much as their parents did.

Carol (Karima) Parry

This plate is glazed in apricot and is made from a Harlequin blank. It was made by Jonathan as he began developing test colors for the future post 86 Fiesta line. This is one of the plates he and his family used in their home as part of their everyday china. NEV (**N**o **e**stablished **v**alue).

Introduction

I am an unabashed Fiesta™ collector.

Somewhere in Iowa, long ago, in the sweet perfumed shade of rustling lilac bushes, during lazy summer days at grandpa's farm, we children would sit solemnly, and sometimes not so solemnly, the ice clinking in our drinks as we sipped our strawberry Kool-Aid served from grandma's Fiesta gray disk pitcher. I can't really remember what we talked about, or the games we played. I do remember the warmth and the sweetness, and how happy we were to all be together; and I remember grandma's Fiesta gray pitcher. The other pieces were brighter, of course. We loved grandma's many colored plates with her famous "Lost Recipe" tea cakes. And sometimes we would fight over which color plate we wanted with a sliver of warm cherry pie and homemade ice cream. But of all the pieces I remember, with their various shapes and colors, there was just something magical about the gray pitcher.

Today, that pitcher sits in a place of honor in my own Fiesta collection. Today, I have a lot more Fiesta than my grandma could even imagine existed. So many shapes, so many colors, and in the middle of it all, the old gray pitcher. It was so long ago that it poured strawberry Kool-aid, but it is still so magical. I never have to fill it, and it never runs dry of the sweet happy memories of long ago.

I'm not really certain when I became a genuine Fiesta collector. But I do remember, many years ago, when I was made aware of it. My three year old daughter and I were out shopping and exploring new thrift stores. As we entered one such store, my daughter suddenly started tugging at my sleeve, "Mommy, Mommy, look," she cried out, pointing towards a display against the wall, "Fiesta!" We had become a four generation Fiesta family. Fiesta truly was an old family friend.

In June of 1999, I decided to take my love of Fiestaware to a new level by writing a book about it. I knew there were already other very good books out there on the subject of Fiesta, but I wanted to write a book not just about the dinnerware, but about the people involved in making the dinnerware, and also about how the dinnerware fit into people's everyday lives. I contacted Jonathan Parry, the art director at the Homer Laughlin China Company (HLC). Jonathan thought my book was a great idea and agreed to offer any assistance he could. From that initial contact arose a close working friendship that continued when I became involved in yet another book project, as one of the contributors to the recently published *Fiesta, Harlequin, & Kitchen Kraft Dinnerwares*, The Homer Laughlin China Collectors Association Guide, published by Schiffer. This book has quickly become a standard for collectors.

A family reunion in 1961. I'm the first child on the left, seated by my grandmother's Fiesta pitcher.

Chapter 1

Jonathan

Growing Up

Jonathan's parents, Dorothy and Elvid Parry. *Photo courtesy of Gene-Ellen Walton.*

Jonathan Owen Parry was born August 31, 1948, at Michael Reese Hospital in Chicago, Illinois. Shortly after his birth, Jonathan's mother, Dorothy Walton Parry, moved her two children to Manchester, Connecticut, and divorced Jonathan's father. Tragically, when Jonathan was only four months old, his older brother, Arthur, died from a bacterial heart infection. Jonathan and his mother spent several years living at his grandparents' home and then moved to nearby Berlin, Connecticut. Jonathan recalls that his father, Elvid Parry, was never involved in his growing up.

Although Jonathan would eventually become a master ceramic designer, his mother's influence would lead to his first artistic love — the design and making of fine jewelry. When Jonathan was seven years old, his mother, an artist and teacher, enrolled in a gem cutting class. Jonathan would watch in wonder as Dorothy practiced cutting and polishing gems at home. Feeding his innate curiosity, Dorothy bought her son a book about gems and minerals, and the two of them attended local rock and mineral shows and exhibits. By the time Jonathan was twelve, Dorothy had also learned how to make silver jewelry. One day to entertain himself while his mother was out for the day, Jonathan decided to try his hand at the jewelry making process. He had watched his mother making jewelry but had never taken a formal course himself. When his mother returned home, he presented her with a gift, a small silver ring which his mother treasures to this day.

By the time he was a Sophomore in Berlin High School, his mother was working as a lab technologist in a local hospital. When he was out of school, Jonathan would often visit his mother at work. Dorothy had many mother and son talks with Jonathan in which she expressed her hope of how wonderful it would be for him to become a doctor. It was during this time, and seemingly with no explanation, that Jonathan's grades began to drop at school. Baffled, Dorothy had another mother and son talk about his grades. After some discussion it was determined that there had been a big misunderstanding about Jonathan's future. Jonathan, feeling that his mother had her heart set on his becoming a doctor, and not wishing to confront her outright, had been sabotaging his grades so that he couldn't get into medical school. After some coaxing, he timidly confessed to wanting to be an artist. Dorothy told Jonathan that she fully supported his dream of becoming an artist, and his grades turned around. He graduated from Berlin High School in 1966.

Jonathan's 1966 High School graduation picture. *Photo courtesy of Dorothy Tims.*

Jonathan when he was two years old. *Photo courtesy of Dorothy Tims.*

Artistic Influences

Jonathan applied for entry to five art colleges; his applications were accepted by four. He decided to enroll in the Tyler School of Art at Temple University, Philadelphia, Pennsylvania. His undergraduate studies were greatly influenced by the artistic talents of his friend, Albert Paley, who had only recently received a graduate degree from Temple University and was already developing a reputation as an artist on the cutting edge. Jonathan's own love of Art Nouveau style inspired the whiplash curves that were to become a trademark of his jewelry. Jonathan received his bachelor's degree in fine arts in 1970.

After graduating from Temple University, he was accepted into the prestigious master's program at the School for American Craftsman at the Rochester Institute of Technology (RIT), Rochester, New York. As Jonathan started working towards his Master's Degree, he was already versed and immersed in the traditions of the Arts and Crafts Movement started by John Ruskin and William Morris in the late nineteenth century. One of the basic tenets of the Arts and Crafts Movement was that there need be no separation between fine art and applied art. Everyday items of use could be made, and should be made, as artistic creations and, as such, the artisan's point of view was critical in the production of such everyday items. Consumer goods could be not only functional but esthetically pleasing. Within this framework, manufacturers could produce objects which were not only profitable, but also artistic.

While a student at RIT, Jonathan studied under the watchful eye of Hans Christensen, an old world Arts and Crafts silversmith from Denmark, who insisted his students learn strict, traditional artistic techniques.

As part of the curriculum, Christensen required his students to make items for a silver coffee service, including a spout for a coffee pot and creamer. At the time, Jonathan didn't see any relevance in this requirement. "It's the 1970s and people don't want to buy a silver coffee service anymore," argued Jonathan. Christensen was unyielding, and so Jonathan made the silver service. However, after Jonathan received his grade for the project, he decided that he wanted to find more useful purposes for the coffee service set. He took the spout for the coffee pot and turned it into the handle for a cane. He sealed the end of the spout that would have attached to a coffee pot with a sheet of metal and added a black, carved walking stick with slight twists in its design resembling flowing coffee. Jonathan then focused on the creamer, which was quickly converted into an incense bowl. The bowl was round at the top and transitioned to an oval shape at the bottom (something Christensen liked to see in silver pieces). Sporting a lid and two spouts, one on each side of the piece, the bowl's handle attached to the creamer's pedestal legged base. Then, creating a foot for the pedestal base by casting something that closely resembled a large chicken foot with red enamel nails, he added it to the creamer's pedestal leg. When a cone of incense was placed inside the piece and lit, and the lid was in place, smoke poured from the spouts on either side of the lid. It was one of the few surrealist pieces Jonathan ever produced, but still he felt that the new creations were more relevant than an old fashioned silver coffee service.

Jonathan and Christensen were often at odds with each other. But even though the conservative teacher and his unorthodox student disagreed on more than one occasion, in the end Christensen taught Jonathan to be a rigorous craftsman, while at the same time learning to appreciate Jonathan's emerging talent. In 1972, when Jonathan was a second year graduate student, he created a hand mirror that Christensen felt was an amazing artistic creation.

Jonathan had employed classic French-Belgian Art Nouveau whiplash curves to accentuate a glass hand mirror. The mirror was in the shape of an oval, tapered on one side to resemble the shape of an eye. When used, the reflection of the viewer's eye became the jewel setting at the center of the mirror, completing the mirror's concept. Christensen felt the mirror was so good that he entered it in the Lever House exhibit sponsored by major world silver companies, where it won an award. Jonathan had not even been aware that his teacher had entered his mirror in the exhibit. This was the first major public validation of Jonathan's work. Jonathan received his Masters Degree in fine arts in jewelry and metal smithing in 1972.

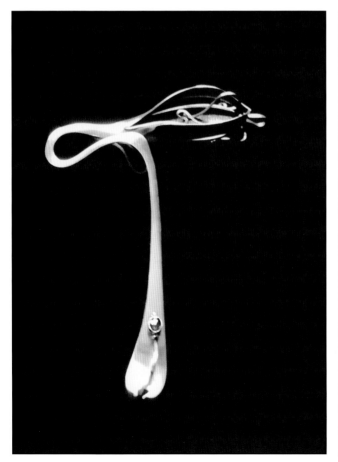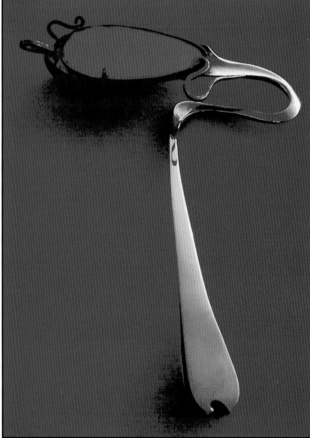

Front and back views of the hand mirror that was entered in the Lever House exhibit. *Photos courtesy of Parker Parry.*

The Homer Laughlin China Co.

While working on his Masters Degree at RIT, Jonathan met his future wife, Carol Ruth Ornitz. Carol was the daughter of a company director at the Homer Laughlin China Company and the great-great granddaughter of Louis Aaron who, along with his sons Marcus and Charles, had purchased part interest in HLC in 1898. After a lengthy engagement, the couple was married at her parent's home, Robert and Ruth Friedman Ornitz, in Pittsburgh, Pennsylvania, on July 5, 1974.

At the time of his marriage, Jonathan was teaching art in the Norwalk Public High School, Norwalk, Connecticut, and he also taught evening classes at Quinnipiac College (now Quinnipiac University, Hamden, Connecticut). A year later, at the invitation of his father in-law, Jonathan accepted a job at HLC on September 2, 1975. Friends said he was very excited about going to HLC. Aware of the company's history, and as a long time admirer of Fredrick Rhead, he took the job hoping to use his creative talents to design items for everyday use in the Arts and Crafts tradition.

After arriving in Newell, West Virginia, Jonathan faced an uphill battle to convince everyone that he was qualified to work in the ceramics industry. Facing the stigma that he was there just because he married an Aaron, Jonathan went to work in the art department under the direction of Dennis Newbury. Mr. Newbury recalled that, when Jonathan worked as a designer in the art department when he first arrived, his designs were way ahead of their time. Mr. Newbury added that HLC's customers were main stream, middle of the road distributors, and Jonathan's new and innovative ideas were not quite what they were looking for. It was also during this time that Jonathan, as well as others, started thinking about reintroducing Fiesta to the market place. Mr. Newbury said many in the industry thought that Fiesta would have been welcomed back with open arms by consumers, but HLC was hesitant. Times were tough in the pottery business and, without a customer, cash in hand, willing to place a large order, HLC didn't feel comfortable making the investment that would have been required to bring it back into production. Like other companies at that time, they felt they needed to conserve their resources. Carol Parry told me that Jonathan had been secretly developing test colors during that time, hoping that someday, Fiesta would be reintroduced. She said, "He made a set of dishes using old Harlequin blanks and some of his test glazes. We used them as our everyday dishes. I also thought the time was right to bring back Fiesta and I often urged Jonathan to go to my great uncle, Marcus Lester Aaron, and ask him about bringing Fiesta back, but despite my nagging he was reluctant to do so. Finally, one day he did approach my great uncle, who was opposed to the idea, and the matter was dropped."

In part because he wanted to learn more about the production end of the business, and because he felt that his ideas and designs weren't being taken seriously, Jonathan left the art department and took a job as a foreman in the decorating department. Although he felt creatively stifled at work, his personal life was on an upswing. On January 28, 1982, a day Jonathan always described as the happiest day of his life, Jonathan and Carol welcomed their newborn son, Jonathan Parker Parry, into their lives. Parker would be their only child.

In 1983, when Dennis Newbury left HLC, he went to management and strongly suggested they consider Jonathan as the next art director. He recalls, "Jonathan Parry was a great talent. At that time HLC needed someone to shake up the place and make changes in the way things were being done. I knew he could do the job." Some in the community said it was another instance of nepotism, but the Wells and Aaron families recognized Parry's unique talents and gave him the position — one of the smartest business decision they ever made. Jonathan became the new art director of HLC in 1984.

In 1985, Jonathan began working closely with Bloomingdale's on the reintroduction of Fiesta. While his professional life was flourishing, his marriage ended. The divorce was amicable but many couldn't understand why he didn't leave the family business after his marriage ended. Privately, he told Carol that he still had a strong sense of loyalty to the Aaron family and the business but publicly he simply stated, "I was happy working at HLC, so I stayed." He finally found an avenue where he could fulfill the vision of the Arts and Crafts movement, producing high quality, functional items that were artistically designed and readily available to the public.

During his career at HLC, Jonathan was known within the pottery community for more than just his Fiesta designs. He led the design restoration of the four original patterns of the Colonial Williamsburg plates unearthed in Williamsburg, Virginia, during archaeological excavations. These plates were the original patterns used during the 1700s in the four most popular taverns in Williamsburg. For HLC's institutional and restaurant customers, Jonathan designed the company's current shapes, including Gothic, Seville, Royale, Lyrica, and Normandy. The Society of Glass and Ceramic Decorators (SGCD) sponsors the annual Discovery Awards competition to recognize outstanding decorated ceramic and glassware designs and technical achievements. In 1993 and 1994, Jonathan and the HLC art department produced award winning plates that were featured on the cover of the SGCD's magazine. The 1993 plate, designed by Jonathan for Foxwood Casino in Connecticut, simulates the look and texture of hand-painting by using a ten color, inglaze decal. The pattern on the plate is called Pompeii. The 1994 plate's mosaic design featured turquoise and lapis to create a palm and lotus motif, while the center featured King Tut surrounded by shades of gold. Done for Empress Casino in Joliet, Illinois, as a sample, the plate that was eventually produced for the casino was in brown and pink.

During his tenure as art director at HLC, Jonathan was always guided by his belief that HLC customers wanted to buy beautiful, well designed products. Carol said that Jonathan often stated that a badly designed piece cost the same to produce as a well designed one and that, when given a choice, the buying public would choose the better designed piece. Jonathan worked with HLC customers, teaching them about design concept and convincing them to invest their money in beautifully designed products. By using his creative talents and the principles of the Arts and Crafts Movement, Jonathan created artistically designed objects that brought HLC even more success in the American pottery industry.

Mr. and Mrs. Robert Arthur Ornitz
announce the marriage of their daughter
Carol Ruth
to
Mr. Jonathan Owen Parry
on Friday, the fifth of July
Nineteen hundred and seventy-four
Pittsburgh, Pennsylvania

Jonathan and Carol on their wedding day. *Photo courtesy of Dorothy Tims. Wedding invitation courtesy of Carol Parry.*

Jonathan shortly after his marriage to Carol in 1974. *Photo by Carol Parry and courtesy of Parker Parry.*

Jonathan and Parker in May of 1982. *Photo courtesy of Dorothy Tims.*

Jonathan and Parker in 1986, the year Fiesta was reintroduced into the marketplace. *Photo courtesy of Dorothy Tims.*

Jonathan in the art department in 1999.

1993 SGCD Discovery Award plate. This plate appeared on the cover of *The American Ceramic Society Bulletin* in December 1993. NEV.

1994 SGCD Discovery Award plate. This plate appeared on the cover of *The American Ceramic Society Bulletin* in December 1994. NEV.

12

Jonathan, Collecting, and Collectors

Part of Jonathan's art glass and pottery collection displayed in his family room.

Jonathan always had a special fondness for Fiesta collectors because he was an avid collector himself. He learned about collecting antiques from his mother and developed an eye for beauty at a young age. It was through his mother and her collections that he learned about Art Nouveau and the American Arts and Crafts Movement. Throughout his life he collected many art objects, but some of his favorite pieces were made of glass. He displayed his art glass collection in the family room of his house, including some examples of Tiffany Glass.

Jonathan's other collections also reflected his interest in Fredrick Rhead. Rhead, a member of a prominent English pottery family and the originator of Fiesta dinnerware, became interested in the Arts and Crafts Movement early in his career. After arriving in America, he eventually became an acclaimed artist in the American Arts and Crafts Movement. Carol remembers that even before Fiesta's reintroduction into the marketplace, Jonathan studied everything he could about Rhead and collected books and articles about Rhead and his family. Jonathan displayed his Rhead collection at the Homer Laughlin China Collectors Association Convention in 1999, winning the HLCCA Gold award. He displayed his award, a cobalt blue disk pitcher decorated with a decal bearing the name of Fredrick Rhead, proudly in his living room at home. His collection represented the wide-sweeping influence of the Rhead family in the art world.

The Jewelry Business

During the years Jonathan was involved in the development and marketing of Fiesta, Fiesta 2000, and other popular HLC lines, he continued to focus his creative talents on designing fine jewelry. When working on commissioned pieces, he never asked his clients what design they wanted, only the type of metal, gems, and style they preferred and how much they wanted to spend. He told friends he never let clients tell him what to make, saying, "I'm afraid someone would ask me to make a poodle pin with little red ruby eyes." He decided a long time ago not to make jewelry for a living client because he didn't want to have to compromise his art to keep clients happy. Throughout his career, Jonathan received many prestigious awards for his jewelry and metal smithing talents, including the Purchase Award Goldsmith, Smithsonian Institute, Washington, DC. This award winning piece was later acquired by the Minnesota Museum of Fine Art and exhibited in its gallery. His works were part of worldwide exhibits, including the Creative Jewelry Exhibition at the Culture Center Complex in Manila and the First World Silver Fair in Mexico City. In 1978, he won the Fashion Jewelry Award in the Diamonds Today Competition held in New York City. The ring he entered was his wife's wedding band, set with a row of nine irradiated diamonds forming a spectrum from yellow to dark orange. In an interview published in the February 10, 1983 edition of the *Pittsburgh Press*, he said, "I really like tailored jewelry that won't go out of style, like Chanel suits." He said he thought of his jewelry as art, adding, "I find it to be wearable art. Even small jewelry is very sculptural. I don't mind working within restrictions. It's good problem-solving. Some people find it objectionable, but I don't. I don't feel you have to have unlimited boundries to create." As a member of the Society of North American Goldsmiths, his works were reviewed in many trade journals, including *Craft Horizons, Contemporary Jewelry, Casting and Jewelry Craft, Metal Jewelry Techniques,* and *Who's Who in the Jewelry Industry.* Jonathan continued to create fine jewelry up to the time of his death. His last commission was for a member of the Aaron family.

Stricken with cancer and knowing his prognosis was poor, Jonathan concealed his condition and continued to work as the art director of HLC until he died. However, he considered himself a very lucky man, saying, "When most places find out you're sick they get rid of you. Joe (Joe Wells III) said I can continue to work as long as I want to." Near the end, he was able to work only a few hours a day. People who knew him said he didn't go to do business, but to be close to his friends. The members of the art department weren't just his friends, they were his second family. And Jonathan told me he hoped he would be remembered simply, "...as a good father and a good friend."

Jonathan Parry died at his home on April 28, 2000. His family, and hundreds of friends and colleagues, came to his funeral as the entire town mourned his passing. At the end of the memorial ceremony, hundreds of post 86 Fiesta colored balloons were released in tribute to his memory and, as they drifted over the HLC factory, the people below stopped, watched, and remembered a great man whose impact on design and upon the American Pottery industry will be felt for years to come.

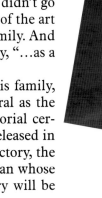

Silver ring by Jonathan Parry. Circa 1969. *Photo courtesy of Parker Parry.*

Gold ring with stone. Made by Jonathan Parry. Circa 1969. *Photo courtesy of Parker Parry.*

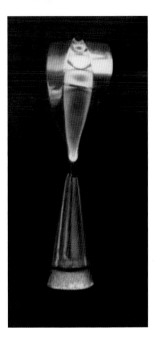

Silver and gold riding switch. Circa 1972. *Photo courtesy of Parker Parry.*

Silver dessert casserole by Jonathan Parry. Circa 1972. *Photo courtesy of Parker Parry.*

Silver and pearl pin by Jonathan Parry. Circa 1972. *Photo courtesy of Parker Parry.*

Silver and gold necklace with black and white pearls, onyx, and chrysophrase by Jonathan Parry. Circa 1973. *Photo courtesy of Parker Parry.*

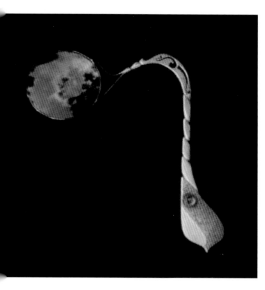

Magnifying glass—silver with moonstone by Jonathan Parry. Circa 1974. *Photo courtesy of Parker Parry.*

Jonathan enjoyed making creative boxes. This work, entitled Stride Box, is made of silver, gold, and ruby. Notice the chicken feet. Circa early 1970s. *Photo courtesy of Parker Parry.*

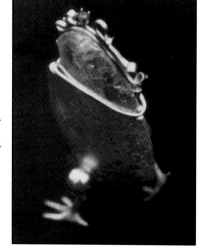

Lock and key silver and gold box with W/70 ct. star garnet by Jonathan Parry. Circa 1974. *Photo courtesy of Parker Parry.*

Lady's evening clutch bag by Jonathan Parry. Silk, silver, and purple stone. Circa 1974. *Photo courtesy of Parker Parry.*

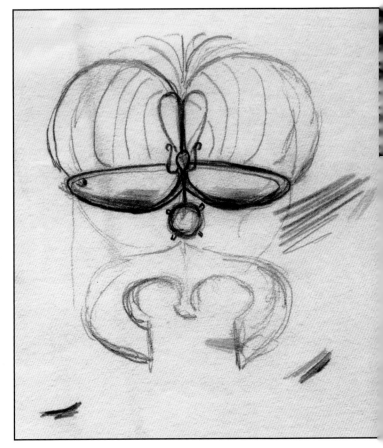

Jonathan also enjoyed making masks. Sketches by Jonathan Parry. *Photo courtesy of Parker Parry.*

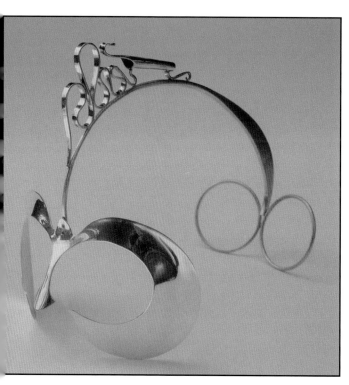

Mask Royale by Jonathan Parry. Circa 1991.
Photo courtesy of Parker Parry.

Silver mask adorned with a peacock feather
by Jonathan Parry. Circa 1974. *Photo courtesy
of Parker Parry.*

Royal Iris by Jonathan Parry. Silver, pearls, and
purple stone. Circa 1991. *Photo courtesy of Parker
Parry.*

A model wearing a mask made by Jonathan adorned with a peacock feather. Side and rear views. Circa 1973. *Photo courtesy of Parker Parry.*

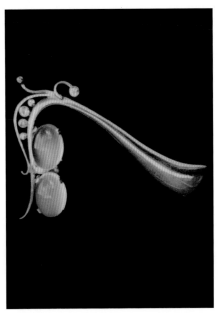

Gold pin with silver moonstones and diamonds by Jonathan Parry. *From the collection of Carolyn Olbum. Photo by Carolyn Olbum.*

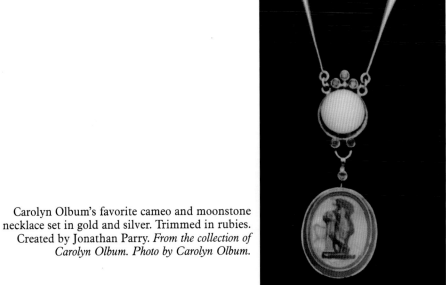

Carolyn Olbum's favorite cameo and moonstone necklace set in gold and silver. Trimmed in rubies. Created by Jonathan Parry. *From the collection of Carolyn Olbum. Photo by Carolyn Olbum.*

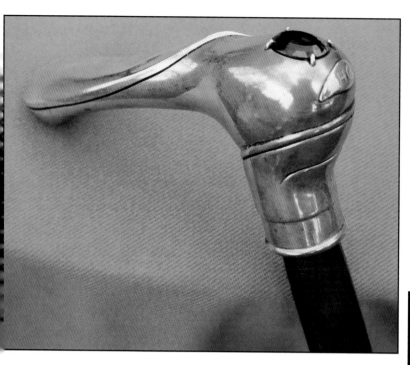

Silver cane handle with blue stone by Jonathan Parry. Circa 1992. *From the collection of Carolyn Olbum. Photo by Carolyn Olbum.*

The collaborative work of Jonathan Parry and Carolyn Olbum. Cast pendant. Gold and pearl. Circa late 1980s-early 1990s. *From the collection of Carolyn Olbum. Photo by Carolyn Olbum.*

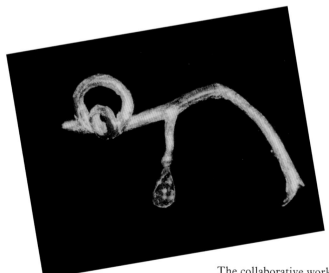

The collaborative work of Jonathan Parry and Carolyn Olbum. Cast gold pin and stone. Circa late 1980s-early 1990s. *From the collection of Carolyn Olbum. Photo by Carolyn Olbum.*

Chapter 2

The History of Post 86 Fiesta

Changing Times in the Ohio River Valley

In the late 1960s and early 1970s, the country, in the middle of a recession, faced hard times, but nowhere were times harder than in the Ohio River Valley, the heartland of the American pottery industry. Faced by fierce foreign competition, rising costs, and changing tastes in the marketplace, sales dropped, causing many US china companies to fold and leaving local economies devastated. The region became so poverty stricken that the US government gave the area Appellation status, entitling the residents to special federal government relief.

Pottery owners in Ohio and West Virginia asked federal politicians to pass an act that would create protective tariffs by taxing imported pottery. After a study by the US government, their request was denied. The government advised the industry owners that, if they wanted to survive, they would have to become more competitive in the marketplace. In its bid to become more competitive, HLC laid off workers and introduced cost saving measures at the plant, including increased mechanization. During the resulting labor unrest, workers sabotaged clay, disrupting production lines. Others destroyed company property, including an incident where workers overturned a company truck and pushed it down a hill behind the factory.

Adapting to changes in the market place, HLC officially retired Fiesta on January 1, 1973.

Welcoming Back an Old Friend—The Reintroduction of Fiesta

The Homer Laughlin China Company reintroduced its Fiesta line on February 28, 1986, during a ceremony at The Cultural Center in Charleston, West Virginia. The dinnerware line was unveiled in a stately ceremony attended by the governor of West Virginia, Arch A. Moore Jr., along with HLC officials and West Virginia Department of Culture and History officials. Guests and patrons present at the ceremony could buy sets of the newly reintroduced Fiesta at The Cultural Center Shop and those who did received a First Day certificate issued with each set.

When asked why HLC discontinued Fiesta, Jonathan referred to the 1960s and 1970s as "Fiesta's ugly period" and cringed when talking about the Antique Gold and Turf Green colors produced during that time. He said, "The (Fiesta) shape was pretty old by then, and the Harvest Gold and Avocado Green pretty much killed everything. The whole china industry nearly folded. A lot of companies went out of business. Imports grew and business dropped off." Consumers wanted something new and

so began the thirteen year hiatus in Fiesta production.

In the early 1980s, Bloomingdale's was trying to climb out of the country's recession and began a new marketing strategy to raise its shaky sales. Buying the rights from Russell Wright's family, Bloomingdale's began a project to reintroduce Russell Wright China into the marketplace. Planning to attract customers with an upscale line of dinnerware, it began looking for a manufacturer to produce its wares. Like so many others, Stuebenville, the original producers of the Russell Wright China line, had gone out of business so Bloomingdale's approached HLC with its project idea. Records show that in 1985 a few Russell Wright test pieces were produced but because of the enormous costs involved in developing an exclusive line for one chain of stores, the line was never developed. As Homer Laughlin's art director, Jonathan suggested that if Bloomingdale's wanted to reintroduce a classic dinnerware, Fiesta was the perfect choice.

Seeing the economic advantages, Jonathan recognized the time was right to reintroduce Fiesta. Prices for imported pottery were rising, making it harder for foreign producers to dramatically undercut the price of domestic pottery. Jonathan also knew that if Bloomingdale's elected to use Fiesta, the startup costs would be lower because HLC already had the molds. In addition, he recognized that American dining habits were changing. By 1986, the Baby Boomers, now adults, were setting up households and raising their families. They enjoyed a more casual life style than that of their parents and they wanted dinnerware with a fresh look. During an interview Jonathan said, "In 1986 there wasn't any solid color dinnerware. It was the right time in the market to bring back something with a retro feel. Today, people talk about the real pale pastel Fiesta colors. But you have to remember in 1986, those were not pale pastels. As a matter of fact, they were considered just slightly, tastelessly bright. People were getting away from formal dining. It became much more casual. Fiesta filled the need."

Besides being beneficial for Bloomingdale's, HLC management knew they would also greatly benefit from the reintroduction of Fiesta. Looking for ways to decrease startup costs, Bloomingdale's agreed to a plan where they would hold exclusive rights to the product for a time and reintroduce the Fiesta line into the marketplace. After that HLC would then be able to market the line to other dealers. At the last minute, HLC decided to make its post 86 line from vitrified clay, enabling the company to also sell Fiesta as part of its food service line. Once Bloomingdale's made its final decision to commit to the plan, the HLC art department began work on the product's development.

Certificate of First Day Issue. *From the collection of Charles Hall.* NEV.

THE HOMER LAUGHLIN
CHINA COMPANY:
A *Fiesta* OF
AMERICAN DINNERWARE

A FIESTA OF FACTS

THE HOMER LAUGHLIN CHINA COMPANY:
A FIESTA OF AMERICAN DINNERWARE

WHEN:
March 9, 1985, to March 1087
Presented by the West Virginia Department of Culture and History

WHERE:
West Virginia State Museum at The Cultural Center
State Capitol Complex
Charleston, West Virginia 25305

WHAT:
An interpretative exhibit of the world's largest pottery, The Homer Laughlin China Company, with hundreds of pieces and the history of its rich heritage. One-time producer of more than 33 percent of the nation's china, the company has been a leader in design and production for over a century. The popularity of the Fiesta line lives on today with generations of collectors.

LAUGHLINS MAKE HISTORY
The story begins with the young enterprising Laughlin brothers, whose innovations in white ware production competed successfully with British imports in the 1870s.

The Company outgrew its 32-kiln operation in the Ohio Valley pottery center of East Liverpool, Ohio, and in 1904 moved across the river to Newell, West Virginia. The first 10-acre plant could produce 300,000 pieces of finished pottery a day. By the 1920s, the company had two-and-a-half times the capacity of any other pottery in the world. And, by 1940, production reached 7,544,078 dozen pieces, roughly one piece of ware for each 1½ persons then living in the United States.

Innovative management brought in the finest engineer and designer, creating a dynamic team in the 20s that perfected mass production of high quality ceramics at affordable consumer prices.

FABULOUS FIESTA:
FIESTA! The bright colors and design of these fabulous everyday dishes cheered a De-pression-weary nation, and continued to be produced for 37 years. A rainbow of Fiesta fills the exhibit and shows the variety of markings found on the dishes, focuses on the collecting craze and Fiesta as art, and spotlights rare pieces and popularly-collected items.

TODAY'S COMPANY:
The Homer Laughlin China Company, in its second century of production, draws upon its tradition of quality. The emphasis is development of new china lines with the Company's design heritage in mind. Today, the pottery produces a strong line of hotel and restaurant tableware.

The reintroduction of the 1986 line of Genuine Fiesta Dinnerware portrays the company's belief in the future of American-made ware.

PRESENTED BY THE DEPARTMENT OF CULTURE AND HISTORY, THE CULTURAL CENTER, CHARLESTON, WV

Facts sheet and price list from the post 86 exhibit presented by the Department of Culture and History, The Cultural Center, Charleston, West Virginia.

THE HOMER LAUGHLIN
CHINA COMPANY:

A *Fiesta* OF
AMERICAN DINNERWARE

PRICE LIST

5 Pc. Place Setting
   (dinner plate, salad plate,
    cup, saucer, soup cereal bowl)
	$15.00

Round Platter	6.00
Serving Bowl	4.00
Large Disk Pitcher	9.50
Small Disk Pitcher	5.40
Covered Sugar & Cream with Tray (set)	11.80
Individual Covered Sugar	5.80
Individual Cream	4.10
Covered Teapot	11.20
Sauceboat	8.40
Covered Casserole	16.50
Round Candlestick	2.50 ea.
Salt & Pepper Shakers (set)	2.20
Covered Coffee Server	10.30
Pyramid Candlestick	3.40 ea.
Medium Vase	15.00
Bud Vase	2.50

PRESENTED BY THE DEPARTMENT OF CULTURE AND HISTORY, THE CULTURAL CENTER, CHARLESTON, WV

Post 86 Fiesta—The Tough Stuff

A major difference between vintage Fiesta and its post 86 counterpart is that vintage ware was made from a semi-vitrified clay while the post 86 Fiesta, as well as HLC's restaurant line, is made from vitrified clay. Although every company has their own formula—which is kept as a trade secret—vitrified clay is generally composed of feldspar, quartz, and 40%-50% kaolin. Fritt, ball clay, and alumina are also added in various combinations. Fritt is used to give the fired product a glass-like appearance and while alumina is naturally present in all clay, it is added to hotel and restaurant ware to make it denser, stronger, and shock resistant. Feldspar acts as a flux in the firing process, fusing the other materials in the clay together during the vitrification process. This fusing process makes the final product less porous. When glazed greenware made from vitrified clay is fired in a single firing process,

nal vintage molds had been used, the post 86 plates would have been smaller than their vintage counterparts. Promotional material shows the first post 86 casserole, sugar bowl, teapot, and coffeepot were based on the Ironstone Fiesta design. Because changes were made in the type of clay used, the casserole, sugar bowl, and teapot pictured in the promotional brochures were never mass-produced; however, small numbers of the sugar and creamer in the old Ironstone design were sold before they were taken off the market. Even after Fiesta was introduced into the marketplace, some unforeseen production problems developed that required the art department's attention. The coffee pot and teapot designs had to be modified. When the vitreous clay is fired, it goes into a semi-liquid state that caused certain designs to warp. By making changes in their designs, the art department alleviated the problem. Through the years, the art department made additional modifications to numerous items and added new items and colors to the Fiesta lineup. With its growing popularity, Fiesta remains a work in process.

An example of a post 86 individual sugar and creamer in cobalt blue made in semi-vitrified clay. They were only made for a short period of time and replaced with remodeled vitrified items. *From the collection of Ellie Rovella.* Sugar, $150-200. Creamer, $100-125.

the same process HLC uses in its plant, the temperature in the kilns reach 2300-2400 degrees Fahrenheit. The vitrification process creates a product that is impermeable to liquids. For sanitation purposes, hotel and restaurant ware must meet strict government regulations that define how impermeable to liquids wares must be. The above produces tableware that meets those standards.

When HLC decided to switch from semi-vitrified to vitrified clay, some of the original vintage molds and Fiesta items had to be redesigned. Because vitrified clay shrinks more than semi-vitrified clay when it is fired, the molds used for the post 86 plates had to be modified and made bigger. If the origi-

"Genuine"

FIESTA

exclusive product of

The Homer Laughlin China Co.

Made in the U.S.A.

"Genuine"

FIESTA

THE EXCITEMENT OF FIESTA RETURNS

In 1936, the Homer Laughlin China Company introduced FIESTA dinnerware to the American public. Created by Frederick Rhead, Homer Laughlin's chief ceramic designer, FIESTA combined graceful lines with bright, distinctive colors — creating a casual style of dinnerware compatible with any decor or color scheme.

Available in many beautiful colors and a wide assortment of basic and accessory pieces, an appreciative buying public made FIESTA a best-seller in its field. Even after its production ceased, FIESTA'S continued popularity made it one of the most sought after collectibles on the market.

Now, by popular request, the Homer Laughlin China Company is proud to re-introduce Genuine FIESTA dinnerware...retaining the same graceful lines, in colors designed to complement today's modern lifestyle. Perfect for all occasions, FIESTA dinnerware will complement any decor and add emphasis to any tablesetting.

Though other color-glazed imitations abound in today's marketplace, don't settle for anything less than the original quality and enduring value of Genuine FIESTA from the Homer Laughlin China Company.

FIESTA...the dinnerware that turns your table into a celebration.

COLORS AVAILABLE:

FIESTA ROSE F103
FIESTA BLACK F101
FIESTA WHITE F100
FIESTA COBALT BLUE F105
FIESTA APRICOT F104

Homer Laughlin China Company (HLC) sales brochure announcing the return of Fiesta. Notice the original post 86 coffee server, teapot, casserole, and individual sugar and creamer designs. Coffee server, $200-300; teapot, NEV (no established value); casserole, NEV; individual sugar, $150-200; individual creamer, $100-125. Brochure, $25-30.

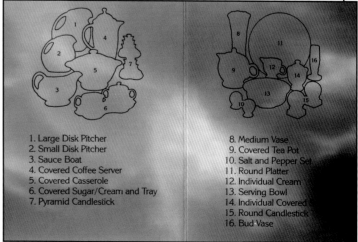

1. Large Disk Pitcher
2. Small Disk Pitcher
3. Sauce Boat
4. Covered Coffee Server
5. Covered Casserole
6. Covered Sugar/Cream and Tray
7. Pyramid Candlestick

8. Medium Vase
9. Covered Tea Pot
10. Salt and Pepper Set
11. Round Platter
12. Individual Cream
13. Serving Bowl
14. Individual Covered
15. Round Candlestick
16. Bud Vase

Colors from the Rainbow—Picking the Fiesta Colors

With all the possibilities, how did the Homer Laughlin art department come up with the first post 86 Fiesta colors? In developing the trial glazes, Jonathan, Ralph Franke (the HLC chemist who helped to create and develop the first nine post 86 glazes) and other members of the art department looked at the emerging trends in the pottery, clothing, and home fashion industries. Jonathan said, "We chose the most current market direction colors that looked right, something people would be comfortable with." Initially, the art department wanted to use gray as a neutral color in the new line, but HLC management vetoed the idea saying Fiesta means "color" and gray is not really a "color." (HLC management later reversed its decision and introduced gray into the HLC Fiesta line in 1998.) After three dozen test glazes were developed, the final five were chosen to go into production; black, white, apricot, cobalt blue, and rose.

As the dinnerware matured, other colors were added to the Fiesta line. When Bloomingdale's asked HLC to include more colors in its Fiesta line, it initially refused, but Bloomingdale's pledged to place large orders for the new colors, prompting HLC to produce yellow in 1987, turquoise in 1988, periwinkle blue in 1989, and sea mist green in 1991. Later, other colors were introduced, including persimmon in 1995, cinnabar in 2000, and sunflower in 2001. In November 2001, word of HLC's new color, plum, made its way to collectors. Colors are added and dropped because of changing consumer tastes. Explaining how styles and tastes change, Parry said, "Cobalt is more popular now than it was in the beginning. It always has been popular in the Midwest but not on the East and West Coasts. Now, suddenly, it's popular everywhere and is one of our top colors." He continued that, "on the other hand, once persimmon was introduced, the sales of apricot dropped dramatically and the popularity of the color declined." Apricot was discontinued in December of 1997. At the time of this writing, other colors slated to be discontinued include pearl gray by the end of 2001 and rose by the end of 2002. According to Dave Conley, the National Sales Manager for Retail Markets at

HLC, at the end of 2000 cobalt blue was still the most popular Fiesta color, followed by juniper and yellow. As for black, HLC says it is on "non-stock" status, which means it is only produced several times a year, requiring a longer lead time for orders. HLC wants to eventually do away with black. Like all Fiesta glazes, black scratches and scuffs and, because of its highly reflective nature, it readily shows imperfections. Jonathan explained, "We would like to discontinue black but we have quite a few hotel customers that buy it and it still remains popular in hollowware so we do it about once a month. We haven't been able to make it go away."

Before a new color is released, HLC does not do extensive color test marketing like other companies. After a color is developed, Dave Conley compiles a list of names for the new color. Then, Jonathan explained, "After everyone puts in his or her two cents, the CEO's wife, Mrs. Joseph Wells III, makes the final name decision."

After Jonathan's death on April 28, 2000, HLC released two new colors, cinnabar and sunflower. Shortly before its introduction, Dave Conley posted a question on the www.mediumgreen.com message board that read, "What does the word cinnabar mean to you?" Collectors quickly responded and the new color was enthusiastically received. Cinnabar was made available to the entire market; however, Bloomingdale's got sunflower as an exclusive color for the first six months, making it a little more difficult for collectors to obtain. As a side note, collectors got a sneak preview of the new sunflower color seven months before it was officially produced. HLC donated a sunflower millennium III vase and dinner plate for an auction to benefit the Homer Laughlin China Collectors Association at its annual conference in June 2000. Afraid a collector would pay a large sum for a plate that would be made available to everyone at a later date, Joseph Wells III signed and dated the back of the plate to document it as a test piece. Since the millennium III vase is no longer in production, this unique item will never be mass produced, making this example an extremely rare piece.

HLC's new color, plum. CRV (**Current retail value**).

26

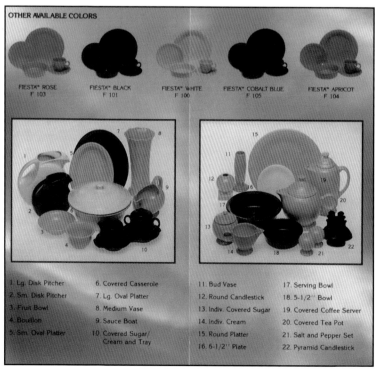

A sales brochure introducing yellow as the newest Fiesta color. $8-10.

Limited Edition Colors

Since Fiesta's reintroduction into the market place, there have been four limited edition colors produced: lilac, 1993-1995; chartreuse, 1997-1999; and juniper, 1999-2001. Sapphire was produced in 1997 exclusively for Bloomingdale's and was limited to only 180 firing days. Jonathan spoke of the reasoning behind HLC's decision to make certain colors for a restricted number of production days. "It's really a marketing decision. We announce the color in advance and you know it's only going to be available for so long. Knowing this, many consumers don't wait to buy the pieces they want." He then added, "We are not trying to make it collectible." By taking a limited run color in and out of production, while maintaining a stable color line, the company allows customers the option to buy extra pieces to give their present set a new look. Another outcome of limited color runs involves production space at the factory. The company simply can't put in a new color without taking one out.

HLC started their innovative limited edition marketing program with the introduction of lilac to the Fiesta line. Jonathan said, "The department stores thought we were out of our minds." He added that when lilac was dropped at the end of its two year run, the Dayton Hudson stores, "had an absolute cow because it was their number one color." When the store insisted the color be continued, HLC refused to bring it back. HLC optimistically told the store buyers the next limited color replacing lilac would be "as hot" — and they were right. Bloomingdale's exclusive on sapphire later led to other exclusive ventures with HLC. Post 86 collectors prize their lilac pieces. Some items, such as the lilac pyramid candle holders, command vintage prices. Hoping that lightning would strike twice, many collectors and dealers stocked up on chartreuse items before the color was discontinued. To date, prices for chartreuse items have not approached the levels of their lilac counterparts. The secondary marketplace was flooded with chartreuse—and price, like everything else in the marketplace, is subject to the vicissitudes of supply and demand.

Shortly after juniper was introduced, Jonathan described the new color to a *Chicago Tribune* reporter as a cross between evergreen and Caribbean blue, adding that all market indicators pointed to blue as the next fashion trend color. He said, "We didn't want a pure blue. We wanted a deep, rich one. It's a very oceanic, deep, rich, transparent blue-green." Dave Conley has commented that, unlike chartreuse which started off with a bang then declined in sales, they expected Juniper would be a strong color for its entire two year run.

Will there be another limited edition color in the near future? Only time will tell. Until then, it remains a tightly held secret within the walls of HLC.

Store Exclusives

Sometimes referred to as "elusive exclusives" by collectors, HLC promotes the sale of its products by offering department stores, its primary customers, exclusive rights to sell particular pieces or certain items in new colors. By using exclusive rights as an incentive, they encourage and reward stores for placing large orders for their products. For example, Bloomingdale's, one of its biggest customers, gets big incentives and rewards like the exclusive rights to items such as the millennium I vase and temporary rights to an exclusive color. Bloomingdale's was the first store to offer sunflower when it was first introduced in 2001. Not only does the program benefit HLC by encouraging stores to place large orders, the stores benefit too. Not even large stores like Bloomingdale's or Macy's can carry every piece of Fiesta offered by HLC. They prefer to order only what they think their shoppers will buy. By having an exclusive, they can target more shoppers, increase their customer base, and, hopefully, increase their sales overall. In the eyes of HLC, the program has been successful in promoting Fiesta. Collectors can find lists of where to find exclusives on the HLC web page as well as on several Internet collector boards.

The black presentation bowl was an exclusive of the HLC outlet store. $25-35.

Successful the Second Time Around

In the end, HLC sales programs and Bloomingdale's gamble paid off. Fiesta was officially reintroduced on February 28, 1986, and, like its predecessor, was received enthusiastically by the American public. Soon after its reintroduction in the marketplace, Jonathan received word from Bloomingdale's that, for the first time in its history, brides were choosing a housewares pattern in the Bridal Registry — Fiesta.

Although HLC will not officially release sales figures, a commercial pottery trade magazine reported that the company's sales were more than 50 million dollars in 1997 and increased by 15% in 1998. In a 1999 article that appeared in the HFN: the Weekly Newspaper for the Home Furnishing Network, a weekly newspaper of home products retailing, Dave Conley said that about 40% of HLC's business comes from Fiesta; 35% of that is from retail sales and 5% from the institutional market.

Now an American icon, Fiesta's popularity among collectors keeps on growing as it keeps making history.

How Fiesta is Made

Taking The Tour—How is Fiesta Made?

It is fascinating to watch pottery being made. If you are in the area, stop by the HLC outlet store and sign up for a tour. Tours are free to the public and are generally given twice a day. Depending on the activity in the plant, the tours can last thirty to sixty minutes. If you take a tour, please be advised that cameras are not allowed in the plant and, for safety reasons, children under ten may not take the tour. Pat Shreve, the manager at the HLC outlet store, also advises visitors to wear their walking shoes because the tour requires visitors to walk about a mile and to climb a lot of steps. The tour takes visitors throughout the plant so they can get a firsthand look at how Fiesta and other HLC lines are made. On occasion, the tours have to be cancelled because of production problems or because of the heat in the factory during the summer months. After the tour, Pat invites the factory's guests to tour the HLC museum. The museum was renovated in 1998 and showcases HLC's rich history.

HLC factory workers begin the process of making Fiesta by adding water to nine dry ingredients and passing the compound through a filter press that removes the excess water. The clay is formed into cakes which are then sent to a plug mill, (a plug mill is a tool that takes air bubbles out of clay), and then sent to various stations and forming machines in the factory.

Some of the clay is piped to forming machines. This is the first stop in the process of making bowls, cups, and plates. After the clay is injected into a mold, it is then raised into an auto jigger machine. While the plaster mold shapes the outside, the machine uses a spinning roller tool to form the interior of the item. The excess clay is "expressed" and the items are removed from the mold, inspected for quality, and placed on the automatic finishing machine. When this process is completed, items are moved by a conveyor to the next workstation where after spending time in a dryer, suction cups place the wares over a hole in the backstamp machine and the items are backstamped. In an earlier process, items were fired, backstamped, glazed, and then fired again. Today, using the latest techniques, they are fired only one time after they are formed, stamped, and glazed, which makes the manufacturing process more efficient.

Items that are flat but not round, like platters, are made in the die ram press. Using plaster dies, a precut section of moist clay is placed on the die press. The press is then closed, forming a platter in a few seconds. After the ware is released from its mold, it is placed in a dryer, backstamped, glazed, and fired.

Slip casting is another technique used to make Fiestaware. Slip is liquid clay and during the slip casting process, liquid clay is piped into plaster molds. When the plaster absorbs enough water, the clay inside the mold takes shape. When the clay is just the right thickness, it is removed from the mold. All Fiesta hollowware, cup handles, and finials are made with this method. When the finished pieces are removed from the mold, they are allowed to air dry. Items that are made from multi-part molds, such as the disk pitcher, have visible seams that require hand finishing. Workers smooth the clay by hand to remove mold marks using moist sponges. Cup handles and finials receive a final trimming after they are removed from their molds. Workers attach the handles and finials to the pottery with a clay base adhesive. Before cups receive their handles, they are backstamped. After the handles are attached, they are placed on rotating shelves of a dryer, then on to large racks and sent for glazing.

The last stop for wares on their way to the kiln is a glazing booth or glazing fountain. HLC started using some lead-free glazes in 1982 and converted completely to lead-free glazes by 1992. Post 86 glazes have always been lead-free. Flat items, such as plates and hollowware with wide openings, like mixing bowls, are sent through the glazing booth. Items are placed on wire stands that constantly rotate while wares are sprayed with glaze from all directions as they move through the booth. After the items are sprayed, workers wipe the feet of the glazed items before they are placed on kiln racks. The kiln racks are stacked and sent for firing. Hollowware, such as the gusto bowl, receives a coat of glaze by way of a glaze fountain. During the two step process, the inside of the hollowware is sprayed using the fountain and then, after it is dry, the outside of the ware is sprayed with glaze by hand.

The last stop for the glazed ware is the kiln. HLC began using a single fire system in 1984 and a single-fast-fire system in 1992. High firing kilns have decreased firing cycles from three days to twelve hours. Since HLC implemented its modernization program, it can ship wares faster than any other American pottery. The modernization program now makes it possible for HLC to make an undecorated product from start to finish within twenty-four hours — one fifth the time of its competitors. Some of the most important pieces of equipment in the one-fire system are the tunnel kilns with an in-line dryer. It was designed to HLC specifications and first installed in the plant in 1992 with an additional two kilns installed between 1997 and 1998. The new kilns are twice as wide as the old kilns HLC installed in the 1920s. The fiber-lined kilns are 265 feet long and 12 feet wide. Stacks of wares are brought to the tunnel kiln by railcar and, after the firing process, the wares are transferred from the exit end of the kiln to the return track. They are then taken to another processing area and placed on a belt which feeds a foot polishing machine that deposits them on a rotating table from which they are selected and packed. The kiln car track system is computer controlled. A main kiln control room, or station, is located between the one-fire kiln and the high fire decorating kiln. This room is elevated, making all kilns visible from this station.

Another type of kiln used is the circle kiln. The circle kiln is shaped like the letter "C". While the cars of the kiln are in constant motion, workers stationed at both ends of the kiln work loading and unloading wares at the same time. Thanks to such innovative manufacturing methods, HLC can produce wares quickly, increasing productivity while decreasing the cost of production.

Lead Free Decorating

After the ware has gone through the foot finishing process and selection stations, it can be packaged for sale or put aside to be decorated. There are two types of decoration used at HLC: high temperature inglaze and low temperature overglaze decorations. Inglaze processes include silk screening, decal application, and color lining which can be applied by a machine or by hand. Inglaze decals, either purchased or made by HLC, are placed on wares by hand and refired at cone 4 (about 2000 degrees Fahrenheit) in a fiber-lined kiln in a five-hour process. The decal sinks into the glaze, giving the final product a smooth feeling and, because the decal can't scratch off, the ware is dishwasher and microwave safe. All decorated post 86 Fiesta produced by HLC is made with inglaze decals. This includes items sold through Mega China, the HLCCA exclusive juice pitcher series, and all decaled post 86 Fiesta tableware items sold in major department stores.

All new products start here in the HLC art department.

A sign at the HLC factory.

A souvenir plate given to those who take the tour by HLC. $3-5.

HLC continues to update their facilities, providing their customers with the highest quality products available in the marketplace today. *Factory brochure courtesy of HLC.*

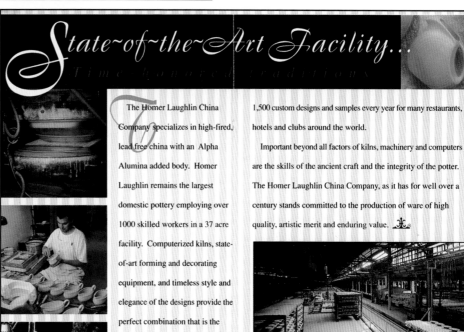

State~of~the~Art Facility...
Time~honored traditions

The Homer Laughlin China Company specializes in high-fired, lead free china with an Alpha Alumina added body. Homer Laughlin remains the largest domestic pottery employing over 1000 skilled workers in a 37 acre facility. Computerized kilns, state-of-art forming and decorating equipment, and timeless style and elegance of the designs provide the perfect combination that is the hallmark of The Homer Laughlin China Company.

As a leader in the china design and manufacturing market, Homer Laughlin has pursued the issues that affect the market: lead-free product, glaze abrasion, contemporary design and timely delivery. In preparation for the future, Homer Laughlin China has made many provisions to guarantee its ability to serve its customers.

Along with continual development of new, innovative proprietary shapes, Homer Laughlin's award-winning design staff creates over 1,500 custom designs and samples every year for many restaurants, hotels and clubs around the world.

Important beyond all factors of kilns, machinery and computers are the skills of the ancient craft and the integrity of the potter. The Homer Laughlin China Company, as it has for well over a century stands committed to the production of ware of high quality, artistic merit and enduring value.

Visitors to Homer Laughlin China can view the actual manufacturing process from clay to kiln to finished product. Plant tours can be arranged at the Retail Outlet daily.

LEAD FREE IN OUR SECOND CENTURY

31

Is it Old or New—How to Tell if Fiesta is Vintage or post 86

How NOT to Get Ripped Off

The other day I went into a local antique shop to buy a little gift for myself. Being a fanatical Fiesta fan, I scanned the shelves searching for a new piece to add to my ever growing collection. Across the room I saw the familiar Art Deco shape of a Fiesta disk pitcher. With my heart racing, I casually walked over to the shelf (I didn't want the shopkeeper to think I was overly anxious so maybe he'd give me a better deal) and stopped dead in my tracks. Prominently displayed on the dealer's shelf sat an anniversary disk pitcher set in persimmon — with a price tag of three hundred dollars. When I asked the dealer about the price he proudly said the set was vintage and in mint condition. He then pointed to the HLCCA book about Fiesta on his counter saying, "That's the book price." I asked, "What makes you think it's a vintage set when it's not a vintage color and is clearly an anniversary set?" Undaunted, he said he had gotten it from an estate sale adding, "The woman was *very old* when she died." Disgusted, I turned to walk out the door but not before saying, "Mister, that lady may have been old but that set isn't. It's post 86."

Most antique dealers are honest people. Dealers depend on their good reputations to stay in business; however, with Fiesta becoming a highly priced collectible, unscrupulous people, out to make a quick buck, are trying to dupe novice collectors. With a little practice, it's not hard to tell Vintage Fiesta from its post 86 counterpart.

Vintage Fiesta items were made from a semi-vitrified clay that is different from the vitrified clay used in today's production. Items made from the more porous semi-vitrified clay are lighter and more fragile. Vitrified clay shrinks more during firing so new ware made from an original mold will be slightly smaller than it's vintage counterpart and less fragile. Semi-vitrified clay is fourteen percent more porous than vitrified clay, making it more absorbent. Although I don't recommend you do this, (it's not tasty or sanitary) one way to tell if an item is made from semi-vitrified clay is to turn it over and place your tongue on the unglazed foot. If your tongue sticks a bit — it's vintage.

Some Fiesta items are easy to identify as vintage or post 86. For instance, a millennium I vase is obviously a post 86 piece but a carafe with a lid is not. Also, small yet noticeable changes in a design can give clues as to whether a piece is vintage or post 86. For instance, look inside a vintage disk pitcher or juice pitcher and you'll see a small dimple where the handle meets the body. In the post 86 version, the dimple is much bigger. If a dimple is large enough to stick your small finger into it, the pitcher is post 86. (Although this works in the majority of instances,

it's not fool proof.) Another example, the vintage demitasse cup, sits on a small pedestal foot while the post 86 demitasse does not.

Production methods have changed throughout the years and can also give clues as to the age of an item. To tell if a round or pyramid candle holder is vintage, look inside the item. Vintage candle holders were dipped and glazed inside and out. Post 86 items are sprayed, leaving the inside of the item virtually untouched.

Since 1986, HLC has used a rubber backstamp to mark some of its post 86 Fiesta items. Like the old stamp, the new stamp, used mainly on cups and bowls, uses the words "HLC USA" and "genuine," but the new stamp's appearance is different. Vintage Fiesta backstamps use a small "f" in the word Fiesta. The new stamp uses a scrolled capital "F" in the Fiesta name. Then in 1992, with the passage of Proposition 65, the words "lead free" were added to the backstamp. Like most other manufacturers, HLC used lead in its vintage glazes. Some post 86 Fiesta items, however, are not marked with a backstamp. Post 86 items made from original Fiesta molds, including the bud vase, 10 inch medium vase, disk pitcher, salt and pepper shakers, gravy boat, pyramid and round candle stick holders, figure 8 tray with creamer and sugar bowl, individual creamer, and individual sugar bowl (excluding the lid) are inscribed in the same way as their vintage counterparts. Since the introduction of pearl gray in 1998, HLC also marked these items with a small raised "H" in an attempt to help stop the confusion over which pieces are post 86 and which are vintage. The markings found on the bottom of some new designs not made from the old molds, like the millennium vases, presentation bowl, and the millennium candle stick holders are unique. Those items have either raised or indented marks. All backstamps are applied by machine. Eventually, HLC plans to backstamp all post 86 pieces.

When collectors look at a post 86 backstamp, they will notice a series of three small letters in the backstamp itself. This is a date coding system HLC has used since the 1960s. The letters "AA" indicate 1986, "BB" indicate 1987, "CC" indicates 1988 and so on. The last letter indicates what quarter of the year an item was made. The letter "A" indicates the first quarter, "B" is the second quarter, "C" is the third quarter and "D" is the fourth quarter. So a backstamp with the letters "IIA" would indicate an item was made during January, February, or March of 1994. A backstamp can indicate when an item was formed but not necessarily when it was completed. After a backstamp is applied, an item can sit on a storage rack waiting for completion. When trying to date an item, the date coding should only be used as an approximation of the ware's age. Sometimes pieces of new Fiesta can be found without a date code. The date code is the first thing that is eliminated if there is not enough surface area to fit all of the information on an item.

The best way to tell if an item is vintage or post 86 is to know the colors of each era. At the time of this writing, Fiesta is made in twelve colors: white, rose, cobalt blue, yellow, turquoise, periwinkle blue, sea mist green, persimmon, pearl gray, juniper, cinnabar, and sunflower. In November 2001, HLC announced their new color, plum. They also announced that juniper and pearl gray would be retired at the end of 2001, and that rose would be phased out during 2002 and retired by years-end. Other retired post 86 colors include apricot, lilac, chartreuse, and sapphire. New collectors can be easily confused by the similarities between some of the vintage colors and their post 86 counterparts. The vintage turquoise can easily be confused with the new turquoise. When looking at the two side by side, however, its evident that the vintage turquoise has a bluer hue while the post 86 turquoise has a slightly greener tone. Vintage cobalt blue is also easily confused by the novice with sapphire blue; however, side by side comparisons also show a difference. The vintage cobalt blue is a deeper, fuller tone of blue compared to sapphire blue. New collectors can also easily confuse vintage yellow and sunflower; however, again, vintage yellow is a darker, fuller tone of yellow compared to sunflower. For many collectors, the easiest colors to tell apart are the vintage and post 86 chartreuse colors. The vintage chartreuse is obviously a darker hue while the post 86 chartreuse is more reminiscent of the "psychedelic" green of the 1960s. By far the hardest colors to tell apart are the two grays because, even side by side, they look very similar. Since pearl gray's introduction into the Fiesta color lineup in 1998, HLC added a small raised "H" to the underside of all Fiesta made from the original molds but, be forewarned, not every post 86 pearl gray item was made from a modified mold containing the "H." The "H" was introduced about the time gray went into production. Many of the early pearl gray items were made from fired greenware that were produced from molds not bearing the new raised "H." The post 86 gray looks more opaque then the heavier steel gray vintage gray.

With practice, telling the difference between vintage items and post 86 pieces becomes second nature. My advice is, when you go shopping, take a good reference book with you. Just in case a dealer wants to quote his or her book, you can whip out yours and check the facts. Doing some basic homework before you shop can save you money, embarrassment, and stress while you build your collection.

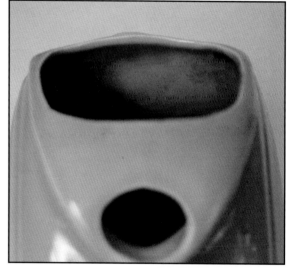

On the top, a vintage disk pitcher with a small dimple where the handle meets the body. On the bottom, a post 86 disk pitcher with a larger, deeper dimple where the handle meets the body.

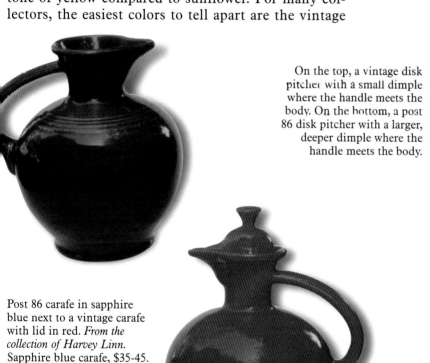

Post 86 carafe in sapphire blue next to a vintage carafe with lid in red. *From the collection of Harvey Linn.* Sapphire blue carafe, $35-45. Vintage red carafe with lid, $300-350.

The vintage demitasse cup on the left, in turquoise, has a hand turned foot. The post 86 demitasse cup, in lilac, does not. *From the collection of Harvey Linn.* Vintage demitasse cup, $70-75. Vintage demitasse saucer, $20-25. Lilac post 86 demitasse cup with saucer, $100-145.

Due to production considerations, many vintage pieces (like this vintage yellow French casserole) were not made for the post 86 line. *From the collection of Charles and Dorothy Morrison.* $275-300.

At first glance, the post 86 pyramid candle holder on the left and the vintage red pyramid candle holder on the right look similar, however, turned over the differences are apparent. The vintage pyramid candle holder has three pin sagger pin marks, a wet foot, and is glazed throughout while the post 86 pyramid candle holder has no sagger pin marks, a dry foot, and is not thoroughly glazed on the inside. Post 86 pyramid candle holders produced since the introduction of pearl gray in 1998 will have a small raise "H" on the bottom, however, not all pyramid candle holders made during the transition in 1998, received the mark. *From the collection of Harvey Linn.* Vintage red pyramid candle holder, $200-300. Cinnabar pyramid candle holders (sold as a pair), CRV.

34

Left: vintage backstamp.
Right: Post 86 backstamp.

A small raised "H" was added to all post 86 items made from original Fiesta molds since the introduction of pearl gray in 1998. However, during the transition, not all post 86 items made from original molds in 1998 received the mark.

The mark on the left is an example of the type VI mold mark found on the post 86 butter dish, platters, Tom and Jerry mug, and teacups. The mold mark on the right, similar to the type IX mold mark, is also used on the post 86 Tom and Jerry mug.

Sometimes dating codes raise more questions then they answer. According to the dating code stamped on the bottom of this lilac casserole, it was made in the first quarter of 1997 but, according to HLC, lilac was discontinued in 1995. Is the code incorrect or were more lilac items produced after 1995? It's just another Fiesta mystery waiting to be solved.

The mark on the left is an example of the type VII mold mark found on 13 inch platters and on new utility trays. The mark on the right is an example of a mold mark found on the utility tray. The scrolled "F" on the platter is almost like a capital "L". The type VII mold mark is the only mark to have this highly stylized scrolled "F"

Fiesta not made from original molds have new mold marks. This is an example of the type V mold mark. It is found on new coffeepots and 6 7/8 inch bowls. Note the letters in Fiesta are not in a straight line. The scrolled "f" is not as smooth and defined as the older version "f" found on vintage Fiesta.

The mark on the left is an example of an indented type VIII mold mark found on post 86 Fiesta mixing bowls. The mark on the right is an example of a raise type VIII mold mark found on the post 86 pedestal bowl and presentation bowl. The lower case "f" on the pedestal bowl is not crossed, making it slightly different from the type VIII mold mark found on the presentation bowl. Notice the circled "R". It denotes that Fiesta is a registered trade mark.

This is an example of a type IX mold mark. It is found on the 2 quart bowl. A variation of this mark is found on the millennium vases.

This is an example of the type X marking found only on the post 86 carafe.

HLC's newest Fiesta color, plum.

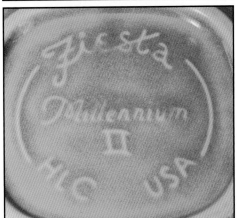

Type IX mold marks found on the millennium I, II, and III vases.

Bottom: Vintage turquoise teacup. $20-25. Top: Post 86 turquoise teacup. CRV (Current retail value).

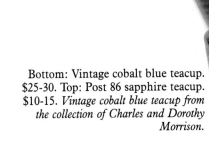

Bottom: Vintage cobalt blue teacup. $25-30. Top: Post 86 sapphire teacup. $10-15. *Vintage cobalt blue teacup from the collection of Charles and Dorothy Morrison.*

Bottom: Vintage chartreuse teacup. $30-35. Top: Post 86 chartreuse teacup. $7-10.
Vintage chartreuse teacup from the collection of Charles and Dorothy Morrison.

A pearl gray teapot lid resting on a vintage gray disk pitcher. $225-250.

A post 86 sunflower demitasse saucer resting on a vintage yellow teacup saucer. Vintage yellow saucer, $5-10. Sunflower demitasse saucer, CRV.

Chapter 3

The Fiesta Line

Through the years, various modifications have been made to a number of Fiesta pieces. Like a plastic surgeon performing a facelift, the modeler may take a slight nip or tuck in an item's appearance involving scant millimeters or, sometimes, because of production problems, make sweeping changes in an item's design. In this chapter you will find pictures of the post 86 line, examples of differences found in various items, and pictures showing differences between vintage items and their contemporary counterparts.

Four piece place setting in plum. CRV.

Plates, Plates, and More Plates

Plates in the post 86 line are based on the vintage Fiesta molds, but because of the type of clay used in their production all the molds were remodeled and made slightly larger to compensate for the shrinkage of the new vitrified clay. There are several ways to tell a vintage plate from a Post 86 plate. For example, there are sagger pin marks on the bottom of vintage Fiesta while the post 86 plate has a dry foot. It is not that unusual to find a vintage plate without a backstamp, since they were stamped by hand and some slipped by production workers. Looking at the plate's backstamp can help determine if an item is vintage or post 86.

Novice collectors can easily be confused between vintage chop plates and post 86 chop plates simply because of their names, but viewed side by side the differences are obvious. Vintage chop plates, introduced in 1936, came in two sizes, 13 inches and 15 inches. The post 86 chop plates are only 11 3/4 inches in size. Made from vitrified clay, the post 86 chop plate is more dense, has a dry foot, and is much less fragile than its vintage counterpart. Like all other vintage plates, the vintage chop plates have sagger pin marks on their underside. With practice, looking for these types of differences becomes second nature to the seasoned collector. The post 86 plates come in a variety of sizes: 6 1/8 inch bread and butter plate, 7 1/4 inch salad plate, 9 inch luncheon plate, 10 1/2 inch dinner plate, and the 11 3/4 inch chop plate.

The snack plate is a new post 86 design and was introduced in 1997 to provide dinnerware for more casual occasions. Designed to be used with the hostess tray, the design of the snack plate is new and found only in the post 86 line.

From the front, it's hard to tell which 7 inch plate is vintage and which one is post 86 but turned over the difference is obvious. The turquoise plate has a wet foot, sagger pin marks, and an old Fiesta backstamp. The persimmon plate has a dry foot and a new post 86 backstamp. *Vintage turquoise plate from the collection of Charles and Dorothy Morrison.* Vintage 7 inch turquoise plate, $5-10. Post 86 persimmon 7 inch plate, CRV.

11 3/4 inch post 86 chop plate in sea mist green on the left. 13 inch vintage light green chop plate on the right. The post 86 chop plate has a dry foot and a post 86 backstamp. The vintage chop plate has a wet foot, sagger pin marks, and no backstamp. Since vintage Fiesta was backstamped by hand, some pieces were missed and did not receive a backstamp. *Vintage light green chop plate from the collection of Charles and Dorothy Morrison.* Vintage 13 inch light green chop plate, $40-45.

Sea mist green chop plate, sapphire blue dinner plate, persimmon luncheon plate, cinnabar salad plate, and black bread and butter plate. CRV.

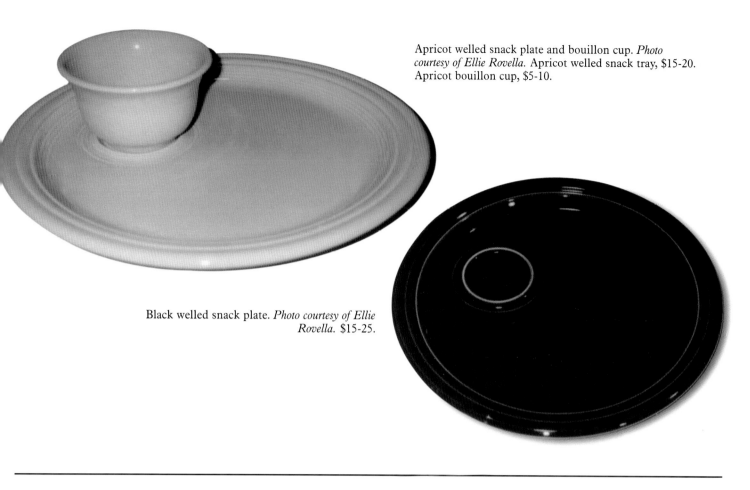

Apricot welled snack plate and bouillon cup. *Photo courtesy of Ellie Rovella.* Apricot welled snack tray, $15-20. Apricot bouillon cup, $5-10.

Black welled snack plate. *Photo courtesy of Ellie Rovella.* $15-25.

Fiesta Serving Trays and Platters

The post 86 Fiesta line offers customers three different size platters, whereas the vintage line only offered one size. Vintage trays are 12 1/2 inches and, like other vintage items, have sagger pin marks on their undersides. Post 86 platters have a dry foot. The post 86 platters are 9 5/8 inches, 11 5/8 inches, and 13 5/8 in size. The post 86 9 5/8 inch platter was made in two versions. The first version is very similar in appearance to the Fiesta Ironstone sauceboat tray and was made from 1986 to 1990. The tray was later redesigned with a flatter bottom, allowing more surface space for food.

The round serving tray, hostess tray, bread tray, relish tray, and pizza tray are designs not seen in the vintage Fiesta line. These new items reflect the new lifestyle and eating habits of the American public. Unlike consumers in the 1930s, nearly every household in America can use a versatile pizza tray. The pizza tray is 15 inches in diameter and though it is the same size as the 15 inch vintage chop plate, the differences can easily be seen when compared side by side. The pizza tray, originally developed for a hotel customer, was introduced in 1999 and remains a very popular Fiesta item. A small number of black pizza trays were made exclusively for Sterns Department Store and are highly prized by collectors. The hostess tray, released in 1997, also reflects a more casual dining style in America today. People are entertaining more in their homes and the hostess tray fills the need of many of HLC's customers. The bread tray, introduced in 2001, was first offered as a Macy's exclusive but was later offered by other stores. The relish tray is also known by collectors as a corn-on-the-cob tray and also as a utility tray and was first mentioned in the HLC modeling logs in October 20, 1994. Although HLC did produce a vin-

Lilac 9 5/8 inch platter, $40-50. Apricot 11 5/8 inch platter, $20-25. Sapphire 13 5/8 inch platter, $30-40. *From the collection of Harvey Linn.*

41

tage Fiesta item called a utility tray, there is very little similarity in their appearance.

The round serving tray is 12 inches in diameter and its design has been slightly changed throughout the years. It was first mentioned in HLC's modeling logs on January 14, 1992. Referred to as a cake plate, it was again mentioned in the logs on August 9, 1994 when the edges around the handles were softened and the imprinted lines on the handle were modified. On November 10, 1995, the logs reflect a desire on the part of HLC to improve the plate, making it lighter and easier to use. One thousand round serving trays were made in sapphire blue and sold through the HLC outlet store during the time sapphire was being sold as an exclusive at Bloomingdale's. In November of 2001, HLC announced that the round serving tray would be retired at the end of the year. As an interesting side note, the modeling logs show that on November 25, 1996, the cake plate was converted into a divided Fiesta vegetable tray. Maybe someday collectors will have a new design to add to their Fiesta collection.

Front and back view of a vintage gray platter. Notice the wet foot, sagger pin marks, and vintage Fiesta backstamp. $60-70.

Vintage red Fiesta utility tray, $85-100. Post 86 chartreuse utility tray, $10-12. *Vintage red utility tray from the collection of Charles and Dorothy Morrison.*

Front and back view of a lilac post 86 13 5/8 inch platter. Notice the dry foot and the lead free post 86 Fiesta backstamp. $40-50.

Post 86 persimmon round
serving tray. CRV.

Post 86 hostess tray in cinnabar and chartreuse.
Cinnabar hostess tray, CRV. Chartreuse hostess tray,
$15-20. The chartreuse tray is shown with a small
serving bowl, $10-15.

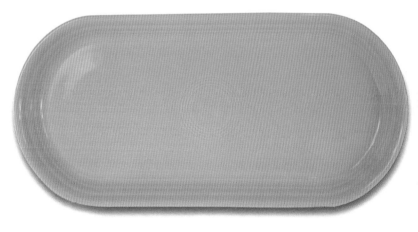

Post 86 sunflower
bread tray, CRV.

The post 86 relish dish, shown in juniper, is also
known as a utility tray. CRV.

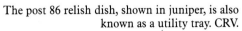

Post 86 pizza tray in periwinkle blue. CRV.

Fiesta Bowls

HLC offers customers a variety of bowls for every need. Some of the bowls have the same vintage name but look completely different. In 1935 HLC began producing its Fiesta nesting mixing bowls and in 1936 its matching lids. There were seven bowls in the set. In March and April of 1994, the post 86 nesting bowls were mentioned in the HLC modeling logs and were introduced later that year. These bowls only came in three sizes and although HLC had planned to develop a machine to produce the matching lids, the project was never completed.

The post 86 rim soup bowl looks very similar to the vintage deep plate but the rim pasta bowl is distinctly post 86. It is interesting to note that when the rim soup bowl was first mentioned in the HLC modeling logs on March 9, 1990, it was referred to as the Fiesta deep plate. Although post 86 Fiesta is generally smaller than its vintage counterpart, this is not the case with the rim soup bowl. When the post 86 rim soup bowl was designed, it was made bigger than the vintage deep plate. The vintage Fiesta soup bowls were more ornate, having handles, and some also had lids. Unlike the vintage soup bowls that were only meant to be used for soup, the post 86 soup bowls are sleeker in design and can be used to serve many different food items. Initially, the rim pasta bowl also had a different name. First noted in the HLC logs on January 3, 1990, it was referred to as the "Fiesta Big Rim

A set of post 86 mixing bowls. $50-75 for the set.

45

Soup" bowl. The name was changed to eliminate confusion between it and the smaller post 86 rim soup bowl and to suggest to consumers another use for their product. Introduced in 1990, these beautifully designed bowls are my personal favorites.

The small, medium, large, and extra large bowls are sometimes referred to as nappy bowls. Nappy is an old English term for an open, earthenware serving bowl. With the introduction of the original Fiesta in 1936, HLC introduced the 8 1/2 inch and 9 1/2 inch nappy bowls. The 8 1/2 inch nappy was made during the entire thirty three years vintage Fiesta was in production. In the 1950s, with the introduction of the "Fifties colors" glazes, the 8 1/2 inch nappies were no longer fired on sagger pins but were produced with a dry foot. The 9 1/2 inch vintage nappies were only produced for eleven years and were all produced using sagger pins. The large post 86 serving bowl is 8 1/4 inches in diameter and, at first glance, looks very similar to the vintage 8 1/2 inch nappy. But on closer inspection, the collector can discern their differences. As previously mentioned, a backstamp or an impressed mark can be used as a tool to help date an item. Also, looking to see if an item has sagger pin marks or dry foot can give clues to an item's age. But remember, the Fifties 8 1/2 inch nappies, like the post 86 bowls, were made with a dry foot, so don't judge the age of a bowl solely on the appearance of its foot. With practice, collectors learn how to tell the difference between vintage ware and post 86 items by color, weight, and overall composition. The post 86 extra large bowl is 10 1/2 inches in diameter and holds 2 quarts. This bowl is similar in size and appearance to the 9 1/2 vintage nappy. The collector can tell the difference between these two bowls not only by noting the difference in their size but also by looking at the rims. The rim on the post 86 extra large bowl is narrower than the rim of its vintage counterpart. The small post 86 nappy is 5 5/8 inches in diameter; just the right size to be used with the hostess tray to hold dips or other relishes; it looks similar to the 5 1/2 inch fruit bowl, but its rim is narrower than the older vintage version. The post 86 medium nappy is 6 7/8 inches in diameter and is the all purpose bowl that comes in the boxed five piece place setting sold by HLC. A novice collector can easily tell vintage and post 86 bowls apart by simply using a ruler.

The covered casserole dish was one of the original Post 86 pieces released when the line was reintroduced. The first test casserole dish was a remake of the old Ironstone casserole dish but, when HLC decided to produce Fiesta using a vitrified clay, its design was modified. Promotional ads show the dish but it never went into full production for general distribution. There are two versions of the post 86 casserole that were produced. The first version has a flat bottom and inside rim while the other has a rounded bottom and no inside rim. The lids for the two casserole dishes are not interchangeable. Viewed without the lid, the new casserole dish is identical to the large mixing bowl. The casserole dish was offered in all the post 86 colors except sapphire.

The stacking cereal, and stacking fruit bowl, bouillon cup, chili bowl, gusto bowl, oval vegetable dish, and the pedestal bowl offered in HLC's post 86 line were never made in the vintage line. In many of today's newer homes, storage in smaller kitchens with fewer cabinets is at a premium. Stacking bowls are a convenient way of using space more efficiently and were offered shortly after Fiesta's reintroduction into the market. The chartreuse stacking cereal bowls were an exclusive of Bloomingdale's. The bouillon cup, added to the post 86 line shortly after its reintroduction, was added to the post 86 line in response to the needs of hotels and restaurants. Its simple, unassuming shape makes it a favorite among many collectors. The gusto bowl, added to the post 86 lineup in 2001, was offered in the Betty Crocker catalog and was also sold in the HLC outlet store. Unlike the 18 oz. chili bowl, the gusto bowl can hold up to 22 oz. The chili bowl, also known as a jumbo bowl, was originally a part of the Fiesta Mate line but, because of its popularity, it became a standard item in the post 86 line. The pedestal bowl looks much different than vintage pedestal-type bowls. The pedestal design was changed because of the newer clay used to make the post 86 pedestal bowl. Because of production problems, the new bowl couldn't be made with the same type of flared base found on vintage bowls. The pedestal on the post 86 bowl is more compact. There were four revisions made to the pedestal bowl before its introduction. The chartreuse pedestal bowl was originally an exclusive of Macys. The oval vegetable dish was introduced in 1999. Many of these bowls fill the bins in the seconds room at the HLC factory outlet. The bowl's large flat bottom makes it prone to glaze imperfections during the manufacturing process.

The presentation bowl was offered to HLC customers in 1997 and was retired from the line in 1999. Referred to as a tri-footed fruit bowl in the HLC design log, six prototypes were modeled before the final design was selected. This highly stylized Art Deco bowl is 11 5/8 inches in diameter and 2 5/8 inches tall. The chartreuse presentation bowl was originally an exclusive of Dayton-Hudson stores; it was offered in black through the HLC outlet store. This design was used to make the 500 raspberry bowls that commemorated the 500-millionth piece of Fiesta made.

The J.C. Penney hostess bowl has quite a history behind its creation. While preparing for the upcoming millennium, HLC's art department was busily designing merchandise for the upcoming event. Noting that the candle business in America was booming and predicting their customers would be buying many more candles in preparation for the upcoming, once in a lifetime holiday event, Bloomingdale's asked Jonathan to design new candle holders just for them. One of the candle holders was a pedestal candle holder. It looked great on paper but after the mold for it was created, its production problems became apparent when they started to crack and warp in the kiln. Not one to throw away a great idea, Jonathan modified the design, turned it upside down, making the top of the candle holder a base for a new bowl. He shortened the sides of the new bowl and created the new Hostess Bowl, available as an exclusive at J.C. Penney.

Also referred to as a deep plate, the post 86 9 inch rim soup bowl, shown in apricot, and its vintage counterpart, shown in turquoise, are similar in appearance, however, on closer examination, several important differences are seen. The post 86 bowl is slightly bigger, has a dry foot, and has a post 86 backstamp. The vintage bowl has a wet foot, sagger pin marks, and a vintage backstamp. *From the collection of Harvey Linn.* Apricot post 86 9 inch soup bowl, $25-30. Vintage turquoise deep plate, $35-45.

Cobalt blue 2 quart extra large bowl, cinnabar 8 1/4 ounce large serving bowl, sapphire blue 19 ounce medium bowl, and chartreuse 14 1/4 ounce small bowl. Chartreuse bowl, $10-15. Sapphire blue bowl, $30-40. Cobalt blue and cinnabar bowls, CRV.

Front and back view of a 5 1/2 inch vintage cobalt blue fruit bowl and a 5 5/8 inch post 86 chartreuse bowl. They look similar from the front but notice that the vintage bowl has a wet foot and sagger pin marks. The post 86 bowl has a dry foot. The rim of the post 86 bowl is slightly narrower than its vintage counterpart. *Vintage fruit bowl from the collection of Charles and Dorothy Morrison.* Vintage cobalt blue bowl, $35-40. Post 86 chartreuse bowl, $6-10.

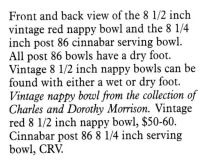

Front and back view of the 8 1/2 inch vintage red nappy bowl and the 8 1/4 inch post 86 cinnabar serving bowl. All post 86 bowls have a dry foot. Vintage 8 1/2 inch nappy bowls can be found with either a wet or dry foot. *Vintage nappy bowl from the collection of Charles and Dorothy Morrison.* Vintage red 8 1/2 inch nappy bowl, $50-60. Cinnabar post 86 8 1/4 inch serving bowl, CRV.

Vintage casserole in light green. *From the collection of Charles and Dorothy Morrison.* $140-160.

Older version of the post 86 casserole in rose. The older version casseroles can be purchased in second hand stores at prices similar to the current retail price of their post 86 counterparts. *Photo courtesy of Arleen Kennedy.*

Post 86 casserole. Shown in persimmon. CRV.

Rose 12 inch pasta bowl, juniper 9 inch rim soup bowl, rose 6 1/2 inch stacking cereal bowl, and juniper 5 3/8 inch fruit bowl. CRV.

Bouillon cup. Shown in chartreuse, apricot, and juniper. Apricot and chartreuse bouillon cup, $5-10. Juniper bouillon cup, CRV.

Chili bowl shown in juniper. CRV.

Gusto bowl shown in persimmon. CRV.

Deep dish casserole shown in periwinkle blue. CRV.

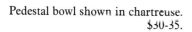

Pedestal bowl shown in chartreuse. $30-35.

Presentation bowl shown in cobalt blue. $35-45.

Hostess bowl shown in yellow. CRV.

Fiesta Mugs, Goblets, Tumblers, and Cups and Saucers

The Fiesta teacup, like so many items, has gone through many changes. By noting a cup's design, a collector can discern an item's period of production. It is very important that collectors be able to recognize the different cup shapes and handle types used by HLC when shopping, especially online. Unscrupulous dealers have attempted to pass off sea mist green and chartreuse post 86 coffee cups as vintage medium green items on e-Bay. The scam goes something like this: A person buys a green post 86 cup and saucer (or any other green post 86 item) at the HLC outlet store in the seconds section for next to nothing and photographs it using a dark green lens filter. They then post it on e-Bay as a vintage medium green Fiesta item. The buyer gets cheated and the seller marks a tidy profit. Knowing this information can protect a collector from getting cheated.

There have been four variations in the Fiesta teacup design. The first Fiesta teacup, made until late 1937, has a flat inside bottom and, like all Fiesta teacups made until the 1960s, had bands of rings inside the cup and had a hand-turned foot. The second variation came at the end of 1937 when the bottom inside portion of the teacup was made rounder and was no longer flat. In the 1960s, the third variation to the cup's design was made. The hand-turned foot was eliminated, the rings were removed from inside the cup, and the entire cup was made bigger.

By the end of the 1960s, HLC streamlined the Fiesta shapes and changed many of the colors to stay current with the times. It was during this time the ring teacup handle was replaced with a "C-handle." During the transition, some of the new "C-handle" teacups were glazed in medium green, turquoise, and yellow. The success of the restyled dinnerware, sold under the names Amberstone, Casualstone, and Fiesta Ironstone, was short lived. The Fiesta line was discontinued in 1973. When Fiesta was reintroduced in 1986, the art department blew the cobwebs off the old "C-handle" cup design and used it in the post 86 line. The post 86 cups and saucers were made in all the post 86 colors. The most valuable colors to look for are lilac and sapphire blue.

The demitasse cup and saucer have been seen by many Fiesta collectors as the "sweetest" items in the vintage and post 86 lines. The vintage cups were put into production in 1935 and were made for approximately twenty-three years. The post 86 demitasse cup was first mentioned in the HLC logs on October 23, 1992, and was made in every post 86 color except sapphire. When assessing the age of a demitasse cup, look at the foot. Vintage demitasse cups sit on a raised foot and the foot was hand-turned. The post 86 demitasse cup doesn't have a raised foot, thereby streamlining the production process and reducing labor costs. Additionally, because it is made from vitrified clay, the post 86 demitasse cup is less frag-

ile than its vintage counterparts. The lilac demitasse cup and saucer, first offered by Bloomingdale's and China Specialties, is highly sought after by collectors and commands high prices. In November of 2001, collectors were notified that HLC planned to discontinue the production of the stick-handled demitasse cup and saucer by the end of the year.

Listed on the HLC web page as the 18 ounce pedestal mug, the latte mug has been a work in progress for many years. Jonathan's former wife, Carol Parry, said that many years ago when the Star Bucks Coffee phenomenon started taking off on the West Coast, Jonathan went to the management of HLC and told them he wanted to design a latte mug. After the meeting, he came home, stormed into their house, and slammed the door. She said, "When he asked HLC about designing a latte cup, management's response was, '....a latte cup, who the hell drinks latte'?" He continued to vent, saying, "I'll tell them who drinks latte—everyone drinks latte!" Of course, in retrospect, he was right and in 1998 he began working on the Fiesta latte mug. Jonathan designed two prototypes before settling on the mug's final design. The first mug, listed as a cappuccino mug, is first mentioned in the HLC log on April 14, 1998. A second prototype, also referred as a cappuccino mug, was listed in the modeling logs on June 3, 1998. This second prototype was eventually released in 2001 as the Fiesta cappuccino mug. The third and final prototype was the present day pedestal mug. Also referred to as the latte mug, it appeared in the logs on October 21, 1998. Many collectors didn't like how the latte and cappuccino mugs were decorated, saying the look was a little too whimsical.

The Fiesta juice tumbler and juice disk pitcher also have quite a history. The vintage tumblers came about thanks, in part, to a business deal that fell through between HLC and Kraft-Phoenix Cheese Corporation. After designing two different sized crocks for the cheese company in 1935, Fredrick Rhead was again approached in 1937 to design other containers for their cheese spread. After countless hours of work, the deal fell through when Kraft awarded the contract to Hazel Atlas Glass. Some time later, Rhead took the design of the cheese jar, modified it, and created the Fiesta juice tumbler. He then took a small disk pitcher that was a leftover prototype from the development of the standard size disk pitcher and created the disk juice pitcher. The tumblers were combined with the pitcher and marketed as a promotional set in 1939-1943. In 1948, HLC introduced the Jubilee line in celebration of HLC's seventy-fifth anniversary and, as part of the new line, the juice pitcher and tumblers were reintroduced in the new Jubilee colors. Then, once again in 1951 or 1952, the tumblers and juice pitcher were used for another promotional. This time it was for

Woolworth's new Rhythm line. In 1995, the tumblers were reintroduced and teamed up with a large disk pitcher in celebration of Fiesta's sixtieth anniversary. The logs indicate the new tumblers were modeled in June of 1995 and then revised in October of that same year. The large disk pitcher was produced from the original vintage mold. When the sets were released in 1996, many collectors grumbled because two of the sets were produced in the retired colors sapphire and lilac. They were afraid that prices for post 86 pieces in those colors would fall if HLC reversed their decision and brought those two discontinued colors back into the marketplace. These sets were also produced in turquoise, periwinkle, cobalt, rose, and persimmon. Rose sets are very difficult to find because only about three hundred of these sets were produced. It is unclear how many sapphire sets were produced but their production was limited to only 180 days. HLC also produced a white Looney Tunes™ anniversary set featuring Tweety Bird™. The tumblers continue to be produced as individual items and as part of disk pitcher sets sold by J.C. Penney's and Bloomingdale's. The J.C. Penney's set features the Fiesta dancing girl on the pitcher. The sets come in three colors: chartreuse, yellow, and pearl gray. The tumblers are also sold as part of a carafe beverage set available through the Betty Crocker catalog.

The post 86 Fiesta mug is listed in the HLC modeling logs on May 19, 1987. The entry indicated that the body of the mug was redesigned but the handle was produced from the vintage Tom and Jerry handle mold, first produced by HLC in 1936. The vintage mug has a slightly different shape than the post 86 mug. The post 86 cups were produced for general retail sales in all the post 86 colors except sapphire.

The jumbo cup and saucer are not truly Fiesta but were part of the HLC restaurant line. Known to collectors as part of the Fiesta Mates, the restaurant ware is dipped in Fiesta color glazes. However, because these items are so popular with many HLC customers, they can now be found on the HLC web page as part of the Fiesta line. The sapphire blue jumbo cup and saucer were made for Bloomingdale's.

The Fiesta goblet is a recent newcomer to the post 86 Fiesta line. An exclusive of Bloomingdale's, it went into production just as chartreuse was being phased out. Collectors scrambled to get their orders in and then the wait began. Production problems hampered HLC's ability to fill the orders. The HLC log indicates that on April 21, 1999, the goblet was made approximately 1/8 inch shorter to stop cracking on the piece during production. Other production problems included the glaze pooling in the bottom of the goblets. Bloomingdale's offered its customers a set of four goblets, all in the same color, for $59.00. Many collectors wanted a variety of colored goblets for their collections but found them too expensive. Instead of ordering multiple sets, some collectors went online and offered to swap goblets with other collectors. The goblets were made in cobalt, yellow, rose, turquoise, persimmon, periwinkle, pearl gray, and, yes, collectors did get their goblets in chartreuse. The JG on the bottom of the goblet are the initials of Joseph Geisse IV, the head modeler at HLC. Occasionally, Mr. Geisse adds his initials to the bottom of some items he modeled. The goblets were also scheduled to be discontinued at the end of 2001.

Vintage cup and saucer shown in medium green. Medium green is described as "John Deere" tractor green by many collectors. It's has a deeper, more vibrant hue then the post 86 greens. Medium green teacup, $40-50. Medium green teacup saucer, $15-20.

Teacup styles have changed throughout the years. The cup on
the left is the second version made by HLC. Notice the inner
cup rings and hand turned foot. The middle cup is the third
version produced. The inner cup rings are gone, the entire cup
is slightly larger and the hand turned foot was restyled. The cup
on the right is post 86. Notice the ironstone handle used on the
post 86 cup. All three cups are shown in turquoise. Vintage
turquoise teacup, $15-25. Post 86 turquoise teacup, CRV.

Post 86 teacups shown in lilac, turquoise, apricot,
yellow, and persimmon. Lilac teacup, $20-35. Match-
ing saucer, $10-15. Apricot teacup, $9-12. Matching
saucer, $5-7. Turquoise, yellow, and persimmon
teacups, CRV. Matching saucers, CRV.

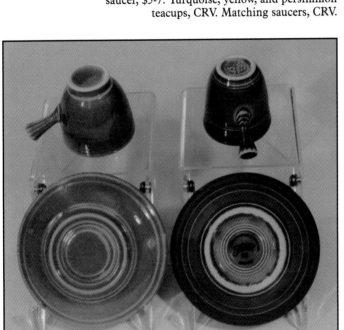

Post 86 demitasse cups and saucers, shown in lilac, have a dry foot. The
cup has an indented mark and the saucer is backstamped. Vintage demitasse cups, shown in turquoise, have a hand turned foot and no marks. The
matching saucer has a wet foot and sagger pin marks. *From the collection of
Harvey Linn.* Lilac demitasse cup with saucer, $100-145. Vintage turquoise
demitasse cup, $60-80. Vintage turquoise demitasse saucer, $20-30.

Post 86 demitasse cups and saucers shown in chartreuse, sunflower, cinnabar, juniper, and apricot. Chartreuse and apricot demitasse cup and saucer, $15-20. Sunflower, cinnabar, and juniper demitasse cup and saucer, CRV.

Latte cup shown in chartreuse. $15-20.

Cappuccino mug shown in sunflower. CRV.

The light green vintage tumbler on the left is smaller than the redesigned rose post 86 tumbler on the right. Light green vintage tumbler, $35-45. Rose post 86 tumbler, CRV.

Plum post 86 Fiesta mug. CRV.

The vintage red mug, also known as the Tom and Jerry mug, lacks the set of rings found on the post 86 mug and has a straighter body than its post 86 counterpart. The handle on the post 86 mug is made from the original vintage mold. *From the collection of Harvey Linn.* Vintage red mug, $70-90. Juniper mug, CRV.

The design of the "Fan Mug," also known as the "Horizon Mug," is put into the surface with a patterned decal that dissolves a layer of glaze during the manufacturing process. They were made as an exclusive for Linen and Things. *From the collection of Deb Ahdoot.* $10-15.

Persimmon jumbo mug and saucer. CRV.

Post 86 goblet shown in yellow. CRV.

Fiesta Salt and Pepper Shakers

Post 86 Fiesta salt and pepper shakers come in two sizes. The table size salt and pepper shakers were designed by Fredrick Rhead and, unlike most items, were made the entire time Fiesta was in production. When HLC started producing Fiesta Ironstone, the design of the pepper shaker was modified slightly when the middle shaker hole was removed. When the post 86 salt and pepper shakers went into production, the original Fiesta molds were used, using the Ironstone modification. Collectors can tell the difference between vintage and post 86 salt and pepper shakers by looking at the bottom of the piece. The old salt and pepper shakers have corks as stoppers while the post 86 items use rubber or plastic stoppers. The new salt and pepper shakers made since the introduction of pearl gray also have an "H" molded into them; however, some of the early post 86 gray salt and pepper shakers do not have a raised "H." HLC added the "H" to post 86 items made from the original molds to help customers tell the difference between vintage ware and post 86 items. The Range Top Salt and Pepper Shakers are uniquely post 86. With home entertaining on the rise and people becoming more creative in the kitchen, HLC added them to their post 86 line in 1997. Their larger handles and overall larger size made them more chef-friendly when cooking. Durable and attractive, they complemented Fiesta kitchen go alongs being produced by other companies at the time.

The persimmon post 86 shaker on the left is slightly smaller than the vintage light green shaker on the right. Vintage shakers have a cork stopper while the post 86 shakers have a rubber or plastic stopper. *Vintage shaker from the collection of Charles and Dorothy Morrison.* Light green vintage shaker, $10-12. Post 86 persimmon shaker, CRV.

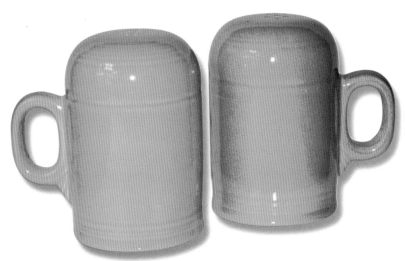

Range top salt and pepper shakers in chartreuse. Pair, $25-35.

Fiesta Sugar Bowls, Creamers, and the Sugar Packet Holder

The Fiesta individual covered sugar bowl design has been through many changes throughout its long and interesting history. The vintage individual Fiesta covered sugar bowl was first introduced in 1936 and was discontinued in 1969. Its ornate design, including its hand turned pedestal foot, scrolled handles, domed lid, and flared finial, make it an easy piece to identify as a vintage item. From 1967 through 1969, HLC produced two covered individual sugar bowls, the classic Fiesta covered individual sugar bowl and streamlined version that was first offered through its Amberstone line. The new version lacked the scrolled handles and elegant hand turned foot. The flared finial was replaced with a smooth, rounded knob. In 1969, when Ironstone Fiesta was introduced, the older covered individual sugar bowl design was dropped. The new streamline design was used because the older shape was dated and the new design was less labor intensive to make. The new design was also used in the Casualstone line that was produced for a very short time in 1970. HLC stopped producing the sugar bowl in December 1972 when it dropped the Fiesta line. In 1986, HLC was planning to reintroduce the Ironstone design but when the decision was made to use a vitrified clay, the design was once again modified because of potential production problems. Using the vintage marmalade mold and removing the notch from its lid, the first post 86 covered individual sugar bowl was made sporting the rounded Ironstone styled finial. Shortly after production began, the Ironstone finial was replaced with the flared finial we find today.

The individual creamer has also seen several design changes. The original vintage Fiesta creamer had a stick handle that matched the A.D. coffeepot, but after only thirty months of production, it was replaced in 1938 with the ring handled creamer. Like the covered individual sugar bowl, it was restyled with an updated look in 1967 using a "C-handle" and introduced in the Amberstone and Casualstone lines. When Ironstone Fiesta was introduced, the restyled creamer was mainstreamed into the updated Fiesta line. In 1986 HLC used the Ironstone individual creamer design in its line. It holds 7 oz. and has had very few modifications to its design.

The sugar and creamer sets, first produced as a promotional item in 1940, were the last wares designed by Fredrick Rhead. In 1986 the set was again produced using the original molds.

Typically, the vintage sets included a cobalt blue figure-8 tray, a yellow handled covered sugar bowl, and matching handled creamer. Some figure-8 trays have also been found in turquoise along with some creamers made in Fiesta red. The modeling logs indicate that throughout the years many slight modifications have been made to the post 86 sugar bowl involving the size and placement of the handles and the type of knob on the lid. The post 86 sugar and creamer set, produced for general retail sales, have been made in all of the post 86 colors except sapphire.

The individual sugar packet holder or sugar caddy was originally a Fiesta Mate but is now considered part of the standard Fiesta line. Made in all the post 86 colors except sapphire, it has been a favorite item of many collectors. When HLC was phasing out chartreuse, it used the last of the chartreuse glaze to make 300 chartreuse caddies that were sold at the HLC factory outlet store's famed sale on October 28, 1999. Limited to only two caddies per customer, they are very desirable pieces in any post 86 collection.

Amberstone individual sugar and creamer in their original packaging. *From the collection of Harvey Linn.* NEV (**N**o **e**stablished **v**alue).

Individual sugar and creamer shown in cinnabar. CRV.

The vintage turquoise individual creamer has a ring handle while the post 86 cinnabar individual creamer has the restyled Ironstone handle. Vintage turquoise individual creamer, $20-25. Individual cinnabar creamer, CRV.

Sugar and creamer set shown in chartreuse. $25-35.

Chartreuse sugar caddy. *From the collection of Harvey Linn.* $25-35.

Fiesta Vases

One of the most popular items in the Fiesta line are the vases. The designs for the bud vase, medium vase, and 8 inch vase come from the vintage Fiesta line. The bud vase, produced in red, cobalt, green, yellow, ivory, and turquoise, was first manufactured around 1935 and was discontinued in 1946. The post 86 bud vase, produced by using the original vintage mold, was part of the original post 86 lineup. The post 86 bud vases have been manufactured in all the post 86 colors except sapphire, though rough sapphire blue bud vases are known to exist. Knowing the colors the vintage and post 86 bud vases were made in is the best way to tell the difference between the vintage bud vases and the post 86 bud vases. Both the post 86 bud vase and the vintage vases have a dry foot. Some of the post 86 bud vases, manufactured since the introduction of pearl gray, will also have a small raised "H" by the Fiesta mark. The lilac bud vase was made exclusively for China Specialties. The vintage 8 inch Fiesta flower vase was made between 1936 to 1944. These vintage vases were produced in red, cobalt, green, yellow, ivory, and turquoise. The post 86 8 inch vase, introduced in 2000 as a Bloomingdale's exclusive, was made from the original vintage mold. First offered in white, yellow, cobalt, turquoise, juniper, pearl gray, and persimmon, they were later offered in sunflower and cinnabar. Since they are made from the original mold and were produced after the introduction of pearl gray, all post 86 8 inch vases also have a small raised "H" on the bottom. The 10 inch medium vase was first produced between 1936 to 1942. These vintage vases were produced in red, cobalt, green, yellow, ivory, and turquoise and had the words "HLC USA" imprinted on the bottom. The post 86 medium vase, produced in all the post 86 colors, also has the words "HLC USA" imprinted on the bottom. The sapphire medium vase was produced for Bloomingdale's. After the vase was produced and during its sapphire exclusive time period, Bloomingdale's arranged with a San Francisco antiques dealer, "Dishes Delmar," to sell them their entire production of one thousand vases. HLC produced several hundred more of the sapphire vases and sold them through their outlet store in 1996. The best way for a collector to know the difference between a vintage 10 inch vase and a post 86 vase is by color because both have a dry foot. Some of the newer post 86 vases made after the introduction of pearl gray will also have a small raised "H" on the bottom of the vase.

The millennium vases are distinctly post 86 items. Jonathan was designing the millennium I vase for general distribution when representatives from Bloomingdale's visited the art department. Seeing the new vase, they claimed it as an exclusive for their stores and a total of ten thousand vases were produced for the Bloomingdale's stores. The design for the millennium I vase is based on the post 86 carafe. The vase was first mentioned in the HLC logs as the "Fiesta 2-Handle vase Millennium series" on July 15, 1998. Initially, the response to the new vase was mixed; however, prices on e-Bay, especially for the chartreuse and pearl gray vases, sky-rocketed. Unfortunately, many collectors felt duped by HLC when the illusion of a "limited edition" vase evaporated with huge numbers of seconds appearing at the HLC outlet store, many in better condition than the ones Bloomingdale's had sold. In truth, Bloomingdale's did only have a limited quantity of vases to sell, but HLC never promised to limit the amount of vases that would be produced overall. Twenty-four black millennium I vases were sold to raise money for the East Liverpool High School Alumni Association. Each of the black vases was marked and numbered for the 1999 event.

When the millennium I vase was taken as an exclusive by Bloomingdale's, Jonathan went about the task of designing another vase for general distribution. When the Macys representatives came to the art department and saw the second vase, they struck a deal with HLC to have it made exclusively for them. The millennium II vase was based on the disk pitcher design and was first mentioned in the HLC log book as the "Fiesta Millennium Disc Vase II" on November 6, 1998. With an unlimited production number, it was made more available and, hence, less expensive. Some collectors didn't like the unusual shape of the millennium II vase. Jonathan explained that when he designed it, he thought about what it would look like holding a tall flower arrangement. He said, "The vase is a single element in the total appearance of the arrangement." Production of the millennium II vase ended in 1999.

Still wanting a vase for general distribution, Jonathan designed the millennium III vase. No one was allowed to visit in the art department when this one was on the drawing board. Resembling a vintage prototype vase, now located in the HLC museum, its sleek Art Deco design was modified and updated in 1999. First mentioned in the modeling log on November 12, 1998, it was produced without a quantity limit, making it easily attainable and modestly priced. FTD Florists ordered a large number of chartreuse vases just before the color was discontinued. China Specialties added a Sunporchdecal to 500 white millennium III vases and offered them to its customers. The HLC factory offered its own exclusive millennium III vase: a pearl gray vase was decorated with a rose decal and sold in the HLC outlet store.

The vintage yellow bud vase is 6 1/4 inches tall. The post 86 juniper bud vase is only 6 inches tall. The best way to tell if a bud vase is vintage or post 86 is by color, otherwise use a ruler. *From the collection of Harvey Linn.* Vintage yellow bud vase, $75-90. Juniper bud vase, CRV.

Post 86 bud vase shown in cobalt blue, chartreuse, sunflower, juniper, cinnabar, and periwinkle blue. Chartreuse bud vase, $12-15. Other bud vases, CRV.

Post 86 8 inch vase shown in cinnabar, juniper, sunflower, and persimmon. CRV.

Post 86 10 inch and 8 inch vase shown side by side. 10 inch sapphire blue vase, $250-300. 8 inch persimmon vase, CRV.

Post 86 10 inch vase shown
in juniper. CRV.

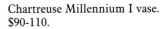

Millennium II vase shown in yellow. $30-35

Chartreuse Millennium I vase.
$90-110.

Millennium I vase shown in persimmon, sea mist green, and pearl gray. $45-50.

Millennium III vase shown in cobalt
blue and chartreuse. $35-40.

Fiesta Candle Holders

It's not a good idea to use the work "dropped" around Fiesta collectors; they break out in a cold sweat and become very queasy. Recently, *that word* brought tears to their eyes when HLC announced its plan to drop the pyramid candle holders from the post 86 Fiesta line. Fortunately for collectors, HLC reversed its decision and on March 29, 2001 HLC made the announcement by posting, "Back by Popular Demand!" on their web page.

The pyramid candle holder, designed by Fredrick Rhead and sometimes referred to as a tripod candle holder, was one of the original Fiesta items released in 1936. Discontinued sometime between 1942-1943, the vintage pyramid candle holders were made in the six original Fiesta colors: red, cobalt blue, ivory, yellow, turquoise, and green. After Fiesta's thirteen year hiatus ended in 1986, the pyramid candle holders returned. Made from the original mold, some novice collectors have problems telling the vintage pyramid and post 86 candle holders apart. Vintage Fiesta is made with semi-vitrified clay and is more porous, making it lighter, more fragile, and a little larger than post 86 pieces made from the original molds. Also, another difference is that vintage pieces are dipped and glazed throughout, and sagger pin marks will be visible, whereas the glaze on the post 86 pyramid candle holder is sprayed on, leaving the inside of the piece untouched. Another difference is that post 86 pyramid candle holders have a dry foot. And if it was produced since the introduction of pearl gray, it will have a small raised "H" on it. HLC did this to make it easier for consumers to tell the vintage items from the post 86. Of course, the best way to tell the difference is by color. Knowing the vintage colors from the post 86 colors can save a collector hundreds of dollars and a lot of grief.

The reissued post 86 pyramid candle holders were made in all post 86 colors except sapphire. And although some rogue sapphire candle holders are known to exist, reissued doesn't necessarily mean inexpensive. Lilac pyramid candle holders, made for only two years as a Bloomingdale's exclusive, are fetching vintage prices on the secondary market. The price for the chartreuse pyramid candle holders have fluctuated. When they were first released, they were in high demand, difficult to find, and prices on the secondary market went through the roof. Now that the demand has dropped and the items are more readily available, prices are stable and much more reasonable.

In 2000, HLC introduced juniper as their fourth limited edition color. Unfortunately for collectors, juniper pyramid candle holders were not made for the full two years. HLC cut short the production of the candle holders, citing falling sales and production problems. HLC stopped production of the juniper pyramid candle holders only after a few months. With that announcement, prices for the juniper pyramids soared on the secondary market. Some sold on e-Bay for upwards of $100. When HLC announced the reintroduction of the candle holders, juniper pyramids were again produced. How this abbreviated production time will affect future prices of the juniper candle holders is unclear at this time.

The round candle holders were first introduced around 1936 and were produced for approximately eleven years. Vintage round candle holders come in red, cobalt, green, ivory turquoise, and yellow. Both vintage and post 86 round candle holders have an in-mold mark on adjacent sides under the square foot. When looking at the vintage and post 86 round candle holders side by side, you will notice that the post 86 candle holder is slightly smaller in appearance due to shrinkage during the firing process and is much less fragile. The lilac post 86 round candle holder was made exclusively for China Specialties while the chartreuse round candle holders were sold as an exclusive at J.C. Penney stores. Part of the original post 86 line, the round candle holder is made from the original mold. Beautiful as well as functional, these post 86 candle holders are available today through many department stores and the HLC outlet store.

Released in 1998, the tripod bowl is only found in the post 86 line. The name "tripod" can be confusing, especially to new collectors. Vintage pyramid candle stick holders are referred to as tripods on vintage Fiesta price lists. The post 86 version is officially listed as a pyramid. The new candle bowl was named tripod because of the three small legs found at the bowl's base. The tripod bowl was designed in response to the rise in the candle market.

The Millennium candle stick holder, also known as the tapered candle stick holder, was designed by HLC at the request of Bloomingdale's. Its highly stylized Art Deco design makes this a stunning piece. Due to advance advertising, the candle holders were popular with post 86 collectors even before they became available to customers. First listed in the HLC modeling log on July 7, 1999, they were introduced later that year. Like the millennium I vase, the candle stick holder was offered in ten colors (they were made available in all post 86 colors except lilac, sapphire, black, and apricot) and limited to 1000 sets each. However, after the rude shock collectors got regarding the large numbers of millennium I vases being sold as seconds, collectors weren't too surprised when they found bins overflowing with millennium candle holders in the seconds room at the HLC outlet store and seemingly more candle stick holders showing up at Bloomingdale's on a regular bases. HLC has always proclaimed that they are not trying to make Fiesta a collectible. They are in the business of turning a profit and providing consumers with quality products at an affordable price. Shortly before his death, Jonathan talked about his plans to design a shorter, plumper version of the millennium candle stick holder for general distribution. Sadly, he passed away before he could work on its design. HLC announced they would be discontinuing the millennium candle stick holder, as well as the tripod candle holder, from the Fiesta line at the end of 2001.

Pair of post 86 lilac pyramid candle holders. *From the collection of Gary and Jeryl Schreiner. Photo courtesy of Gary Schreiner.* $500-600.

Post 86 pyramid candle holders shown in juniper. CRV.

Post 86 round candle holders are made from the vintage Fiesta mold and because they are made with semi-vitrified clay, they are slightly smaller than their vintage counterpart. The vintage cobalt blue candle holder is 3 3/4 inch in height and 2 7/16 inches square at the base. The sunflower post 86 candle holder is 3 1/2 inches in height and 2 3/8 inches square at the base. Since the introduction of gray, post 86 items made from the original mold are marked with a small raised "H". *Vintage round candle holder from the collection of Charles and Dorothy Morrision.* Vintage cobalt blue round candle holder, $60-75. Sunflower round candle holders, sold in pairs, CRV.

Post 86 round candle holders shown in sunflower and cinnabar. CRV.

Post 86 tripod bowl shown in chartreuse. *From the collection of Harvey Linn.* $20-28.

Post 86 millennium candle holders, also known as Y2K candle holders, shown in turquoise. $20-25.

65

Fiesta Disk Pitchers

When it comes to identifying an item as vintage or post 86, many new collectors find the large disk pitchers the hardest item to identify. Not part of the original Fiesta line, the vintage disk pitchers were available from 1938 to 1969. Available in all the vintage Fiesta lines, including Amberstone, Casualstone, and Ironstone, they were made in green, cobalt, red, yellow, turquoise, ivory, rose, forest, chartreuse, medium green, Amberstone brown, and antique gold. The Fiesta logo will not be found on the bottom of the Amberstone brown, or the antique gold disk pitchers. When trying to decide if a pitcher is vintage or post 86, check the inside of the pitcher where the top of the handle meets the body. In a vintage disk pitcher, you will notice a small dimple, but in the new version the dimple is much larger. If a dimple is large enough to stick the tip of your small finger in it, the pitcher is post 86. And any post 86 pitcher made after the introduction of pearl gray, with the exception of some of the early pearl gray post 86 disk pitchers, will have an raised "H" on the bottom. The post 86 disk pitchers are available in all of the post 86 colors. Viewed side by side, the 67 1/4 ounce post 86 disk pitcher is slightly smaller in appearance than its 71 ounce vintage counterpart. Made from the original mold, the pitcher is smaller because the vitrified clay used to make the post 86 line shrinks more during the firing process than the old vintage clay did and although both post 86 and vintage disk pitchers have a dry foot, they differ in appearance. The dry foot on the post 86 disk pitcher is whiter, shinier, and more glasslike than the dry foot on the vintage disk pitcher. The best way to tell if a pitcher is vintage or post 86 is by its color, but, if all else fails, use the tongue test.

As mentioned in the Fiesta tumbler section, the Fiesta juice pitcher was originally a regular disk pitcher prototype that was shelved for about a year before it was resurrected when the juice tumblers were created. The vintage pitchers were made for about four years and are found in red, yellow, harlequin yellow, celadon green, and gray. The post 86 juice pitchers were made for general retail sales in all the post 86 colors except sapphire. Like the regular disk pitcher, the juice pitcher was made from the original mold so, when compared side by side, the 28 ounce post 86 juice pitcher is slightly smaller than its 30 ounce vintage counterpart. Its dry foot is also whiter, shinier, and more glasslike in appearance than the dry foot on a vintage juice pitcher. The gray and harlequin yellow juice pitchers are very similar in appearance when compared to the post 86 juice pitchers made in pearl gray and sunflower. When dating a gray or yellow juice pitcher, check the dimple inside the pitcher where the handle meets its body. Like the regular disk pitcher, if you can stick the tip of your finger in the dimple, the juice pitcher is post 86. Also, look for the small raised "H" underneath the pitcher; but, remember, while all sunflower juice pitchers will have the raised "H," not all of the early post 86 gray pitchers will. Unscrupulous dealers have been known to pass off gray post 86 juice pitchers as vintage pitchers. Relatively few vintage gray juice pitchers were made and they are very valuable. Buyer beware! When investing a lot of money in a prized piece, buy only from reputable dealers and collectors with money back guarantees.

The mini disk pitcher is an individual creamer and was created with restaurants and hotels in mind and was not part of the vintage Fiesta line. This small item is a favorite with many post 86 collectors. Available in all post 86 colors, except sapphire, it is used as a decal item in several China Specialties lines. First found in the HLC modeling log on December 7, 1992, it was introduced shortly thereafter.

Post 86 mini disk pitcher shown is pearl gray and chartreuse. Chartreuse mini disk pitcher, $12-18. Pearl gray mini disk pitcher, CRV.

Post 86 lilac large disk pitcher. $60-80.

Post 86 juice disk pitcher shown in yellow, juniper, apricot, pearl gray, and black. Apricot juice disk pitcher, $15-25. Other juice disk pitcher, CRV.

Fiesta Teapots

Throughout the years, Fiesta teapots have not only been popular with Fiesta collectors but with many general teapot collectors as well. Because of their broad appeal, vintage Fiesta teapots are highly sought after and bring high prices when they are in mint condition.

In 1935, HLC started producing its eight cup Fiesta large teapot. Made for eleven years, it was produced in red, cobalt, green, yellow, ivory, and turquoise. The handles on these teapots are almost identical to those found on the post 86 teapots. The Fiesta medium teapots were made from 1937 to 1969. Made in all eleven vintage colors, they have a "C" shaped handle and are not too difficult to find. In the mid- to late 1960s and into the early 1970s, the medium teapot was used in the Fiesta Amberstone, Casualstone, and Ironstone lines. Produced in antique gold and Amberstone brown, the impressed Fiesta markings were removed and the lid and finial was restyled (although a few vintage medium teapots have been found in Amberstone brown.) The Ironstone teapots were made until December 1972. The Fiesta line was officially discontinued on January 1, 1973.

HLC had planned to use the Ironstone teapot shape when they reintroduced Fiesta into the marketplace but when the decision was made to use a vitrified clay, the teapot had to be restyled. To help keep the vintage look, the old style large teapot handle was resurrected and made its debut when the line was reintroduced. From the very beginning, the new teapot was a production nightmare. Many of the first teapots warped during the firing process. Other production problems directly related to the teapot's design caused many of the teapot's openings to

vary greatly in size. In fact, some of the openings were so large that lids would fall into the pots. In 1994, the art department modified the teapot and the lid to prevent further production problems. Teapots made in the two versions can be found in the following colors: rose, white, black, periwinkle blue, sea mist green, turquoise, cobalt blue, and yellow. To date, there is only a modest price difference between the two versions in the secondary market. Post 86 teapots were made in all the standard colors except sapphire.

When dating a teapot remember that although the handle and finial on the post 86 teapot are similar to that found on a vintage Fiesta large teapot, the lids are quite different. The vintage teapot lid is flatter in appearance while the post 86 teapot cover has more of a dome shape. Another important color clue is to remember that although gray was a vintage color, Fiesta large teapots were discontinued in 1946 and were never made in gray. Several times while checking out e-Bay, I've seen post 86 teapots misrepresented as Fiesta vintage teapots. Being aware of these critical points can help keep the novice collector from making a very expensive mistake when buying a teapot.

First designed in 1996 as a teapot for a children's tea service and later released in the "My First Fiesta" children's tea set, the Fiesta two cup teapot is popular with many collectors. Introduced in 1998, the Fiesta two cup teapot was marketed as an alternative to the Fiesta go along teapots. Released with restaurant and hotel clients in mind, it came out long before the "My First Fiesta" tea set made its debut.

Vintage red large teapot, $230-300.
Post 86 chartreuse medium teapot,
$40-45. Vintage yellow medium
teapot, $140-170. *From the collection
of Harvey Linn.*

Post 86 medium teapot, first version on
the left, and restyled version on the right.
Shown in apricot. Both versions, $30-40.

Post 86 2 cup teapot in yellow.
This teapot is also sold in the
"My First Fiesta" tea set. CRV.

Post 86 2 cup teapot shown in juniper. CRV.

Post 86 medium teapot shown in apricot, juniper, and pearl gray.
Apricot teapot, $30-40. Pearl gray and juniper teapots, CRV.

Fiesta Coffeepots

Also referred to as a coffee server, Fiesta coffeepots are popular with both vintage and post 86 collectors. Designed in the 1930s by Rhead, they first went into production in November 1935. The vintage coffeepots were made for a little over twenty-three years and were made in an array of striking colors including: red, green, cobalt, ivory, yellow, rose, turquoise, gray, forest, and chartreuse. The coffeepot was retired around 1959 but was taken out of mothballs and put back into production with a few modifications in April 1967. The coffeepot's flared finial was replaced with a round knob and, because HLC planned to sell the coffeepot under several different names including Amberstone, Casualstone, and Fiesta Ironstone, the Fiesta marks were removed. During this incarnation, the pots were only made in Amberstone brown and antique gold. When Fiesta was retired in 1973 the design was again shelved. In 1986, the coffeepot made its post 86 debut as part of the original line. The first post 86 coffeepots were made using the old Ironstone design but be-cause HLC had switched to a vitrified clay, production problems occurred. When vitrified clay is fired, it goes into a semi-liquid state so, when the coffeepots were fired, many of them would warp in the kiln and collapse. The new design included a more contoured top which added stability to the coffeepot's design. In addition, the knob on the lid was replaced with a vintage styled finial. These changes appear in the HLC modeling log on March 18, 1986. Since so few of the original designed coffeepots were produced, they are highly prized in the secondary market and are priced accordingly. The post 86 coffeepots were made for general retail sales in all the post 86 colors except sapphire and chartreuse. Twenty four chartreuse coffeepots were made for the East Liverpool High School Alumni Association's charity auction. There are twenty three numbered chartreuse coffeepots known to exist, since one broke in an antique mall after a customer reportedly paid $800 for it. HLC announced its plans to remove the coffee server from the Fiesta line at the end of 2001.

Post 86 cobalt blue coffeepot, CRV. Vintage light green coffeepot, $170-200. *From the collection of Harvey Linn.*

Indented mark on the bottom of a vintage light green coffeepot.

Indented mark on the bottom of an turquoise post 86 coffeepot.

Post 86 coffee pots shown in turquoise, cobalt blue, and apricot. Apricot coffeepot, $30-40. Turquoise and cobalt blue coffeepots, CRV.

The Fiesta Carafe

Although the popular Fiesta carafe appears in both the vintage and post 86 Fiesta lines, that's where the similarities end. Referred to in Rhead's notes and the HLC modeling log as a water bottle, the vintage carafe went into production in 1935 and was discontinued in 1946. Sold in red, cobalt, green, turquoise, yellow, and ivory, the vintage carafe is a "must have" in any vintage collection. When the Fiesta Ironstone, Amberstone, and Casualstone lines were introduced the carafe was retired, but in 1996 a redesigned version of the vintage carafe made its debut in the post 86 line. The new post 86 version had no lid, its neck was wider, and the graceful pedestal foot found on its vintage counterpart was eliminated. The carafe was added to the post 86 line in response to the needs of a food service industry client. The client asked the art department to develop a water container that would accommodate the use of ice cubes. The lid was not included in the item's design because, as Jonathan explained, "It's one less thing to have to wash, store, and replace when it gets lost or broken." The post 86 carafe was "officially" made in all the post 86 colors except lilac; however, a few lilac carafes are known to exist.

The sapphire blue carafe was an exclusive of Bloomingdale's. $35-45.

Post 86 carafe shown in pearl gray, chartreuse, and apricot. Chartreuse and apricot carafe, $35-45. Pearl gray carafe, CRV.

The Fiesta Sauceboat

The sauceboat is one of the few Fiesta items that made the transition to the Ironstone, Amberstone, and Casualstone lines without alterations and, other than the Fiesta marking being removed, is part of the post 86 line today. Originally released in 1937, it was made in all the vintage colors. When the Fiesta line was streamlined, the sauceboat was made in Amberstone brown, mango red, antique gold, and turf green and when post 86 Fiesta was reintroduced into the marketplace, it was one of the first items offered. Side by side comparisons show slight differences in the appearance between a post 86 sauceboat and its vintage counterpart. The new sauceboat, made from the original mold, looks slightly smaller and more stout in appearance then its vintage counterpart and since the introduction of grey, HLC has added a small raised "H" to the bottom of all items made from original molds.

The dry foot on the post 86 sauce boat is also whiter and more glass-like in appearance than the vintage sauce boat. The best way to tell vintage and post 86 sauceboats apart is to know your colors. Many novice collectors have trouble telling the gray and turquoise post 86 sauceboats from vintage ones. After some practice, a collector will be able to notice that the post 86 turquoise has more of a green hue to the color while the vintage turquoise is a truer blue. The color gray is another matter, confusing even the most seasoned collectors. Many post 86 gray sauce boats are marked on the bottom with a small raised "H" but, remember, not all post 86 gray sauceboats have the embossed marking. Made in all the post 86 colors, except sapphire, the sauceboat's classic design remains popular with HLC customers and collectors alike.

The post 86 sauceboat in sea mist green is slightly smaller and heavier than the vintage turquoise sauceboat. Since the post 86 sauceboat is made from the original mold, all sauceboats produced since the introduction of pearl gray in 1998 have a raise "H" on their base. Vintage turquoise sauceboat, $40-50. Sea mist green, CRV.

Post 86 sauceboat shown in juniper, sea mist green, and pearl gray. CRV.

Fiesta Napkin Rings

The Fiesta Napkin Rings are purely a post 86 design. First mentioned in the HLC log on May 21, 1987, they were introduced because of the popularity of entertaining at home and because they would tie in well with some of the planned Fiesta Mate napkins and table accessories. They are very popular with many post 86 collectors and tend to have steep price tags on the secondary market. When the production of chartreuse was scheduled to end, HLC made several hundred sets of chartreuse napkin rings. When word got out that they were going to be sold as an exclusive at the HLC outlet store, collectors clamored to get a set of their own. The napkin rings were sold in every color except sapphire. China Specialties also offered customers Moon Over Miami, Noon Over Miami, and Sunporch Fiesta napkin rings. HLC announced that the napkin rings would no longer be available after the end of 2001.

Post 86 napkin rings shown in chartreuse. $20-30.

Fiesta Butter Dish

The post 86 Fiesta butter dish is another example of how changing times create changing needs in the dinnerware market. In the 1930s when the vintage line was designed, butter generally came in a larger, brick-like shape, not in the stick we find in today's supermarkets. The vintage Fiesta line had no butter dish. With the introduction of the Amberstone and Casualstone lines, HLC introduced the first Fiesta butter dish. This butter dish, however, was shared with several HLC lines and looks much different from today's post 86 design. It does not have a finial, was made in Amberstone brown and antique gold, and both have a mechanically applied decoration in black. The butter dish was not carried in the Fiesta Ironstone line. The post 86 butter dish was first mentioned in the HLC modeling log on March 13, 1992, and was introduced to the public shortly after. The modeling log indicates several modifications have been made to its design. Most notably, the shape of the base was rounded and later on, during production, incised markings were added to the base. Again, in response to the changing needs of their customers, the modeling logs mention a Fiesta butter tub on December 16, 1996 and a matching lid on February 7, 1997. Maybe someday these items will also become available to HLC customers.

Post 86 butter dish shown in chartreuse. $35-40.

Fiesta Lamps

In 1993 J.C. Penney introduced the Fiesta lamp. The lamp, first mentioned in the HLC modeling log on June 23, 1992, was a departure from other Fiesta items in that, although there were vintage Fiesta lamps made (they were made from syrup bottoms and were assembled and sold commercially by another company), this lamp was specifically designed for its purpose and marketed by HLC. Unfortunately, its shape caused production problems, driving the prices higher than the market would support so its length of production was short lived. On August 12, 1997, the teapot lamp was mentioned in the HLC modeling log. Unlike some homemade versions made from modified Fiesta items, this teapot lamp, modeled by Joseph Geisse, is not a teapot base and lid that were glued together, it is one whole piece. Unfortunately, this lamp, too, had a short production run, making it very difficult to find. One raspberry teapot lamp base is known to exist in the HLC art department.

Post 86 lamp shown in black.
From the collection of Harvey Linn.
$125-150.

Post 86 teapot lamp base in periwinkle blue. Base only, $10-12.

Deep Dish Pie Bakers

A favorite of many cooks, the post 86 deep dish pie baker has been a very popular item. First mentioned in the HLC modeling logs on December 20, 1993, it is sold as an exclusive through the Betty Crocker catalog. On June 22, 1994, a small pie plate was mentioned in the modeling log and on July 28, 1994, a medium pie plate was also mentioned. These pie plates were eventually released in the Spring of 2001. The small and medium pie bakers were offered as exclusives of Betty Crocker. Why did HLC wait so long to release these items? It has been speculated that HLC had many new designs being developed for its post 86 line but, with Jonathan's death, much of the new development came to a halt. To satisfy the needs of its retail customers, HLC is pulling out their prototypes and offering them to its big retail customers. The pie plates are available in all the post 86 colors except sapphire, and a yellow pie baker was also produced for the Looney Tunes series. The chartreuse and juniper pie bakers were offered as Betty Crocker exclusives.

Post 86 deep dish pie bakers. 6 inch cobalt blue pie baker, 8 inch turquoise pie baker, and 10 inch cinnabar pie baker. CRV.

Trivet and Spoon Rest Sets

As with the medium and small deep dish pie bakers, the trivet and the spoon rest took a long time to get to the market place. The trivet remained on an art department shelf at HLC since it was modeled on April 8, 1997. Listed as being made for Copco, a company that makes Fiesta accessories, the trivet, according to Jonathan, was originally going to be used as a base for a Fiesta hot plate or as part of an inlaid trivet set. The project never materialized and the prototype was put on the back burner until the buyers from Betty Crocker saw it. A modified version of the prototype trivet was teamed up with a spoon rest that was modeled on October 1, 1999 and was introduced to collectors in the Spring of 2001. The spoon rest project was one of the last that Jonathan worked on before his untimely death. The trivet and spoon rest sets are part of an HLC marketing plan in which they hope to further stimulate the popularity of Fiesta go alongs.

Post 86 trivet shown in juniper. CRV.

Front and rear view of post 86 spoon rest. Notice the scrolled letters "JG" in the rear view picture. They are the initials of Joseph Geisse, the head modeler of the HLC art department. CRV.

The Fiesta Clock

First mentioned in the HLC modeling log on June 29, 1992, the Fiesta clock was introduced into the market place in 1993 by J.C. Penney. It was subsequently removed from production, then reintroduced in 1996 and sold to general retailers as part of the regular HLC line. The face of the clock comes in various shapes including a flat face and a face that looks very similar to a regular post 86 plate. The clocks can appear with or without the sixtieth anniversary logo and, since sapphire blue items were only made for about a year, those clocks are the hardest to find. The chartreuse clocks produced for J.C. Penney were an anomaly. The incident involved the computer system at J.C. Penney not receiving data from the computer programs that the chartreuse clocks were not available from HLC. Without any human involvement, the automatic replenishing program automatically generated an order because there were no chartreuse clocks in stock. That order was received by another computer at HLC. The HLC computer than generated a work order in the plant that the clocks be produced. Factory personnel, believing the order was legitimate, produced and shipped over two hundred clocks in a six month period before HLC learned of the error. HLC announced their plans to drop the clock from the Fiesta line at the end of 2001.

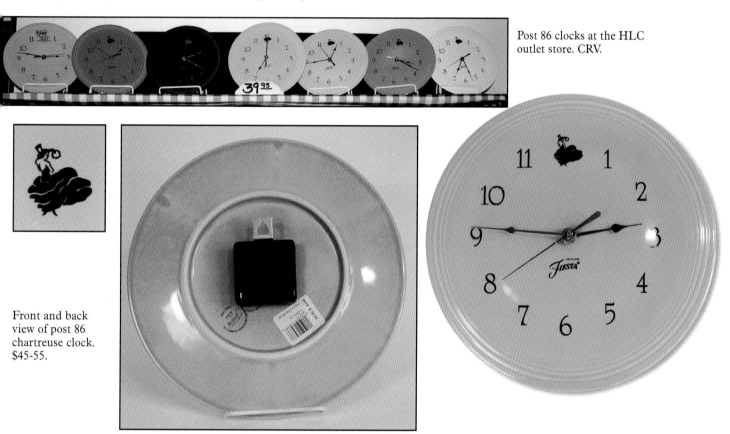

Post 86 clocks at the HLC outlet store. CRV.

Front and back view of post 86 chartreuse clock. $45-55.

Fiesta Tool Crock

The Fiesta Tool Crock was introduced by Betty Crocker in its Fall catalog in 2001. Offered in twelve colors, including juniper, it was welcomed with open arms by many collectors. Described as a larger version of HLC's cappuccino mug, minus the handle and the dancing Fiesta embossments, it stands 6 1/2 inches tall and is 5 inches in diameter. One of the first Fiesta items designed by Judi Noble (who took over as Art Director after Jonathan Parry) and the art department, its practicality made it a hit with Betty Crocker's customers.

Fiesta tool crock. CRV.

Chapter 4

HLC and Decal Fiesta Lines

Aloha Homer: The Lynn Krantz Dishbook Collection

In 1999, Lynn Blocker Krantz had an idea which materialized into Hawaiiana Ware. Formerly a writer for *Bon Appetit Magazine*, she says she always had a passion for everything Hawaiian since she was a teenager. Eleven years ago, while visiting Hawaii with her husband and searching for vintage Hawaiian memorabilia to add to her collection, she discovered the popular menu cover art creation by Eugene Savage. The menu covers were created for the dining rooms of the Matson Navigation Company's luxury liner, SS Lurline. The bright and highly stylized Art Deco designs inspired her to create her HawaiianaWare line. She said, "When I saw a reprint of a Savage mural, I knew immediately I wanted to do something with his images. This new line of dishware is the perfect marriage of vintage collectibles, putting late 1930s artwork on late 1930s dishware."

For many years, the work of Eugene Savage has had its following. Savage, a sculptor, painter, and a professor of painting at Yale, started his six murals of Hawaiian Islands for Matson's menu covers in 1938. Before starting the project, Savage spent three months in the islands studying its history, botany, and native culture. With their completion in 1940, and with the threat of World War II looming over the Hawaiian islands, the eight foot wide by four foot high murals went straight into Matson's San Francisco basement storeroom for safe keeping. The six menu covers finally made their debut in April of 1948. The menu covers, given to the ship's passengers as souvenirs, are in demand by collectors of Hawaiian memorabilia and occasionally surface in second hand and antique stores throughout the United States and on auction web sites. Reproductions of the murals have also found their way onto serving trays, calendars, and Hawaiian shirts. Today, the original murals remain in Matson's corporate headquarters in San Francisco.

Hawaiiana Ware brochure. *Brochure courtesy of Lynn Blocker Krantz.*

Hawaii has always represented the ultimate island paradise, a respite from the headaches, difficulties and trivial problems of everyday life. HawaiianaWare® epitomizes this world of beauty, pleasure and effortless enjoyment of life. HawaiianaWare depicts scenes of Hawaiian pageantry created by renowned artist Eugene Savage. Savage's murals were used as cover art for menus on Matson Navigation Company cruises in the 40s and 50s.

Manufactured by The Homer Laughlin China Company, HawaiianaWare is produced on lead-free, American vitrified china and is oven/microwave/dishwasher-safe. Designs are available in four thematically titled place settings: *Festival of the Sea, Island Feast, Aloha...Universal Word,* and *Pomp and Circumstance.*

HawaiianaWare creates a striking table setting for any occasion, whether casual or elegant.

HawaiianaWare® Patterns & Shapes #8341

Designs

Festival of the Sea

Island Feast

Aloha... Universal Word

Pomp and Circumstance

313 Platter 11 1/2"
315 Platter 13 1/8"
available in "Festival of the Sea"
and "Aloha...Universal Word"

210 Plate 12 1/4"
408 Plate 10 1/4"
407 Plate 9"
available in "Festival of the Sea"

371 Plate 10 5/8"
available in
"Pomp and Circumstance"

288 Saucer 5 3/4 "
available in green palm
(coordinates with all patterns)

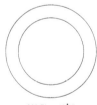
149 Jumbo Cup 18 oz.
available in "Pomp and Circumstance"

197 Jung Bowl 4 1/4" 9 1/4 oz.
available in "Festival of the Sea"

115 Mug 9 1/4 oz
available in "Festival of the Sea" BC# 8342
and "Aloha... Universal Word" BC# 8341

253 Rim Soup 9" 12 3/4 oz.
available in "Island Feast"

484 Disc Pitcher 67 1/4 oz.
available in "Island Feast"

123 Cup 7 oz.
available in "Festival of the Sea"

379 Rim Soup 9 1/4"" 13 oz.
available in "Pomp and Circumstance"

Before she approached HLC about her idea, Lynn did her homework. To see how a mural would look on dishware, Lynn hired a local artist to hand paint part of a mural onto a plate. Amazed at how well her painted plate looked, she then went to a graphic artist and had more mural plates designed on a computer. After putting a presentation together, Lynn met with the director of Public Relations at the Matson Navigation Company in San Francisco and described her concept to him. She recalls that he loved the idea and after getting the company's approval she contacted HLC.

Lynn said she preferred HLC over other companies because it is an American company with a long history and an excellent reputation. After making

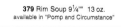

initial contact with HLC, she traveled to Newell, West Virginia, to meet Dave Conley, get a tour of the pottery, and meet with members of the art department. She said that when she met Jonathan Parry and told him her idea, he immediately loved the concept. According to Judi Noble, the present art director of HLC, the average decal HLC uses in its products is made with four colors. HawaiianaWare decals, made in England, utilize eight colors, making them relatively expensive to produce. Jonathan said he was very excited to be involved in the project and even though the decals were expensive to produce, he felt that this exceptional line of dinnerware would be a great success. After a long, painstaking process taking many months, Lynn, Jonathan, and Judi Noble were successful in creating the HawaiianaWare line. The line was introduced at the 2000 Chicago International Housewares Show and became "really hot" in the marketplace. Although, at that time, the Fiesta disk pitcher was the only Fiesta item found in the HawaiianaWare line, many Fiesta collectors obviously also found the new line outstanding. Dave Conley said that the day after HawaiianaWare made its debut on HLC's web page, out of nearly 100 e-mails he received in one day, about seventy percent of them were about the HawaiianaWare.

All HawaiianaWare is make from vitrified clay, making it perfect for use in the home as well as the food service industry. The items not made from the Fiesta line are made using the Ivory Body Product Line. Different shapes used in making HawaiianaWare include the Rolled Edge, Durathin, and Empire. The Rolled Edged is a heavy-duty, wide rim china, Durathin is a medium-duty china with a classic wide rim, and Empire is a heavy-duty china with a coupe shape. Other shapes from the Ivory Body Product Line are available through the Food Service Division at HLC.

HawaiianaWare continues to grow in popularity and has been seen on the set of a popular prime time television show. HawaiianaWare designs include: Festival of the Sea, Island Feast, Aloha...Universal Word, and Pomp and Circumstance. Accompanying the release of HawaiianaWare, Krantz is also publishing a book, *To Honolulu in 5 days - Menus, Recipes and Life Aboard the Matson SS Lurline, 1935-1955.* She hopes to expand her company and create other lines of dishware in association with HLC.

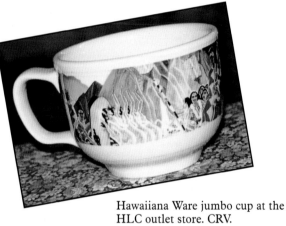

Hawaiiana Ware jumbo cup at the HLC outlet store. CRV.

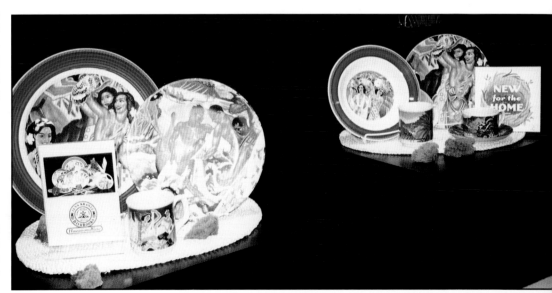

Hawaiiana Ware on display at the 2000 International Housewares Show in Chicago, Illinois.

Fiesta and the American Museum of Natural History

The American Museum of Natural History's exclusive Fiesta collection, featuring beautifully designed space decals, was originally the idea of Paul Murawski, the museum's director and general manager of retail sales and licensing. It was only natural that he would think of Fiesta dinnerware when the museum was looking for items with a retro theme for its new planetarium gift shop in the Rose Center for Earth and Space. Before arriving at the museum, Murawski had been the Director of Gift, Housewares, and Table Top in the corporate buying office for Fedcrated Merchandise and had a long standing relationship with HLC. Along with numerous other projects, he had worked with the HLC art department in the design and development of the millennium II vase, the latte mug, and the presentation bowl — and he loves post 86 Fiesta.

Murawski and the space decal designer, Jennifer Kowalsky, work with the HLC art department in developing the museum's exclusive series of post 86 Fiesta. First in the museum's space decal series was the cobalt blue series featuring the post 86 mug, clock, disk pitcher, bud vase, salad plate, and serving tray. Each series is only produced for one year; but, because of the popularity of the cobalt blue series, three runs of these items were made. Production of the cobalt blue series began in February 2000 and ran through the end of the year. The chartreuse series came next and included the post 86 medium vase, disk pitcher, salt and pepper shakers, salad plate, and serving tray. Production of these series began in October 2000 and ran through the end of 2001. At the time of this writing, the museum plans to make the next series in sunflower. All of the museum's Fiesta items are manufactured with inglazed metallic decals that are made in Germany.

Cobalt blue bud vase and mug made for the American Museum of Natural History. *Bud vase from the collection of Gary and Jeryl Schreiner.* CRV.

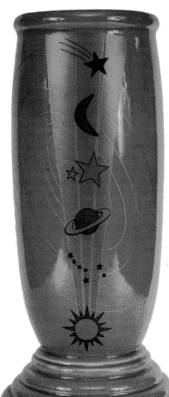

Chartreuse millennium III and round candle holders made for the American Museum of Natural History. *From the collection of Kathy Garrels.* CRV.

Macy's Quatra

Quatra mug. $15-25.

In late 1997, Macy's introduced their Quatra dinnerware. Looking for something that would set them apart, the line was made exclusively for Macy's East and its four underglazed stripes represented Macy's top selling Fiesta colors at the time. Quatra was also available in the "Macy's by Mail" catalog. The Quatra line included a 10 1/2 inch dinner plate, a 9 oz. Fiesta mug, a 14 oz. Bowl, a 7 1/2 inch salad plate, and a 11 3/4 inch chop plate. In 1998, a disk pitcher was added to the line. According to HLC, Quatra was very successful in the marketplace but it took a brief hiatus until its reintroduction in 2001 with the addition of a new pizza tray and oval serving bowl.

Fiesta Christmas Dinnerware

Fiesta Holiday dinnerware is a favorite of many post 86 collectors. Bright and cheerful, it sets a festive tone at any holiday table. In 1987, the first line of Holiday Fiesta was introduced. Made for just one year, this line used a holly and berry decal and was not an overwhelming success. The decal on the next line featured the holly and berry decal with a red, intertwining ribbon. In 1998, HLC gave its salaried employees a red ribbon presentation bowl and, in 1999, a ribbon pizza tray. Available in a variety of items, they are affordable and easily found on e-Bay, the HLC outlet store, and other internet web stores.

HLC also made other less expensive lines for many of their high volume customers. In 1998, Betty Crocker offered its customers a line of Christmas Fiesta featuring a decal with bright and cheery Christmas lights and tinsel. The selection included a mug, dinner plate, and pie baker. Federated department stores offered only one item in 1998, a 9 inch plate featuring a dark blue Fiesta disk pitcher and persimmon Fiesta mug surrounded by a garland of holly. The May Company Stores offered their customers dishware featuring a blue Christmas tree decal. The selection included a mug, dinner plate, and salad plate. The Mercantile Department Store Company offered customers a line of post 86 Fiesta featuring two different decals, one with a multi-colored Christmas tree decorating the rim of a white plate and the other with lights, trees, stars, and ornaments encircling a matching white mug. A dinner plate, luncheon plate, mug, and chili bowl were offered with these decorative designs. In 1999 Betty Crocker again offered its customers the Christmas lights and tinsel decaled ware but with the addition of a luncheon plate. In their 2001 holiday catalog, Betty Crocker's

customers were given additional items to choose from including a large teapot, 11 5/8 inch medium platter, bread tray, spoon rest, large disk pitcher, and deep dish oval serving bowl.

In addition to HLC's children's Christmas dinnerware, including "Cookies for Santa" and "Tis the Season," in 2000 the art department designed the Holiday Window mug. The mug, offered in turquoise, persimmon, periwinkle blue, yellow, white, rose, and sea mist green, was sold through the HLC outlet store.

Another popular Fiesta Christmas item is the Fiesta Christmas tree ornament which HLC has produced since 1997. The ornament is first mentioned in the modeling logs on January 25, 1991. Originally, the art department created two ball-like Christmas ornaments, one plain and one with a strong art deco styling. Unfortunately, they were deemed impractical for mass production and remained in a desk drawer at HLC. The small dish-like ornaments are three inches in diameter and are decorated with the newer holly and ribbon decal treatment on white and the Fiesta dancing lady. The dancing lady ornament comes in four colors: 1997, persimmon; 1998, yellow; 1999, chartreuse; 2000, juniper. In 1999, Judi Noble created her own Christmas ornament featuring Ms. Bea. The Ms. Bea ornament, produced only for one year, was only made in chartreuse. In 2000, HLC produced an ornament made in juniper featuring a white rose and in 2001, white snow flakes. The outlet store had an exclusive Christmas ornament of its own. Featuring a disk pitcher, they were made in persimmon and in white. HLC also made special ornaments for Betty Crocker and the May Company Stores.

The second version of HLC's holiday pattern, commonly referred to as Holly and Ribbon, is still readily available in the following items:

Cup, Mug
Small Bowl 14 1/4 oz.****
Salad plate
Dinner Plate
Round Serving Tray
Large bowl 1 quart
Large disk pitcher
Round candleholder***
Individual creamer
Individual covered sugar
5 Piece place setting
Jumbo cup and saucer**
Teapot**
Range top S&P shakers

Platter 11 1/2 inch
Medium bowl 19 oz.
Luncheon plate
Chop Plate
Saucer*
Miniature disk pitcher
Small disk pitcher
Bud vase*
Salt and pepper shaker set*
Sugar and creamer tray set
20 piece set
Sauceboat**
Welled snack plate

*These items do not have the holly and ribbon decal. The shakers and bud vase have a red line around the base and the saucer has a red edge line.
**New items in 2001
***The candle holders come in two styles, with and without the holly and ribbon decal. The candle holders without the decal are trimmed in red around the edges.
****Listed on the outlet order form as cereal bowl/ candy bowl

An example of the first Christmas decal used by HLC for the Christmas dinnerware line. Cup and saucer, $15-20.

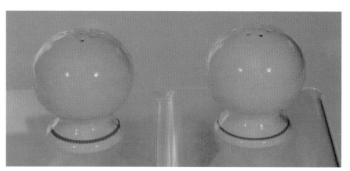

Christmas salt and pepper shakers. *From the collection of Harvey Linn.* CRV.

Holly and Ribbon large disk pitcher, juice pitcher, and mini disk pitcher. *From the collection of Harvey Linn.* CRV.

Holly and Ribbon bulb candle holders.
From the collection of Harvey Linn. CRV.

Holly and Ribbon presentation bowl made as a Christmas gift for salaried employees of HLC in 1998. This bowl is from Jonathan Parry's collection. $300-400.

Holly and Ribbon pizza tray made as a Christmas gift for salaried employees of HLC in 1999. $300-400.

Fiesta 2000 juniper charger with snow flakes. Made as a Christmas gift for salaried employees of HLC in 2000. Signed by Jonathan Parry. $300-400.

Known to collectors as the ginger-bread pattern, this holiday dinnerware line was made exclusively for Betty Crocker. *From the collection of Harvey Linn.* CRV.

9 inch Christmas plate made in 1998 for Federated Department Stores. $10-12.

Christmas mug made for the May's Department Stores. *From the collection of Harvey Linn.* CRV.

Christmas "window" mugs sold at the HLC outlet store. Shown in sea mist green, turquoise, and white. CRV.

Post 86 Christmas ornaments from Jonathan Parry's collection. Notice the ornament on the right does not have a date. $5-10.

1999 Christmas ornament offered through Betty Crocker. *Photo courtesy of Paul Perkol.* $5-10.

Ms. Bea Christmas ornament designed by HLC's present art director, Judi Noble. $5-10.

Warner Brothers Fiesta

HLC was approached by Warner Brothers (also known to collectors as the WB), to produce Looney Tunes Fiesta for the Warner Brothers Studio Store Catalog and for selected WB stores. Jonathan said that working with Warner Brothers turned out to be a major challenge for the art department. Warner Brothers provided the drawings they wanted placed on their wares and it was up to the art department to create the decals that would be used in the final product. When decals are fired onto glazed wares, the colors of decals are altered. The high temperatures of the kilns burn out bright colors like red, turning them into more of a brown hue. The colors of in-glazed decals are also altered when they sink into and blend with the glaze. Warner Brothers wanted their characters to appear in bright vibrant colors, something that is very hard to achieve when producing an in-glazed product. Initially, many samples were made and shipped to a California based company and they were rejected. In the end, HLC added a backing to the decals so that, during the firing process, the colors of the decal and the glaze would not blend together to distort the colors of the decal.

The line was introduced in the summer of 1994 and was sold through the WB catalog and at its flag ship store in New York City. Standard decorations on dinnerware included Scooby Doo on sea mist green, and white, Tweety Bird on white, Porky Pig™ on rose, Sylvester™ on yellow, Bugs Bunny™ on periwinkle blue, and Daffy Duck™ on turquoise. Other specialty items introduced in 1994 included Foghorn Leghorn™ on a periwinkle disk pitcher with Bugs Bunny appearing on the opposite side, Granny™ on a rose teapot, and Pepe Le Pew™ on a sugar and creamer tray set. Other specialty items were added later, including a white 10 inch clock with Bugs Bunny, Tweety, and Sylvester (introduced in 1999), a Tweety 60th anniversary disk pitcher set (introduced in 1997), a white Christmas teapot featuring Tweety and Sylvester, and matching white mugs featuring Tweety (introduced in 1998). HLC also made generic Looney Tunes restaurant ware.

In 2001, the Warner Brothers Studio Store became a casualty of the AOL-Time Warner merger and was shut down in the second quarter of 2001. WB collectors scrambled to get the final remaining pieces before the stores closed its doors. Prices on e-Bay for WB Fiesta have held steady and many post 86 collectors are still interested in expanding their WB Fiesta collections.

Items available in the WB Fiesta series

Tweety "Dewicious!" Series (In white and introduced in 1994)

9 inch rim soup bowl*	tea cup and saucer
10 inch dinner plate*	Large teapot*
coffee mug*	9 inch serving bowl
range top S&P shakers*	casserole (without a lid)**
Jumbo cup (Fiesta Mate)	

*Reissued in 1999
**Introduced in 1999

Bugs Bunny "What's Cookin, Doc?" Series (In periwinkle blues and introduced in 1994)

10 inch dinner plate*	9 inch rim soup bowl*	coffee mug*
teacup and saucer	sauceboat	small disk pitcher**

*Reissued in 1999
**Has Foghorn on reverse saying "Doo Dah, Doo Dah."

Daffy Duck "It's Mine, All Mine" Series (In black and introduced in 1994)

10 inch dinner plate	9 inch rim soup bowl
coffee mug	teacup and saucer
12 inch tab handled serving tray	

Sylvester "Sufferin' Succotash" Series (in yellow and introduced in 1994)

10 inch dinner plate*	9 inch rim soup bowl*
coffee mug*	10 inch pie baker
teacup and saucer	

*Reissued in 1999

Porky Pig "That's All Folks!" Series (in rose and introduced in 1994)

10 inch dinner plate	9 inch rim soup
teacup and saucer	9 inch serving bowl
coffee mug	

Bugs Bunny and Foghorn Leghorn disk pitcher. *From the collection of Harvey Linn.* $65-75.

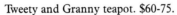

Tweety and Granny teapot. $60-75.

Pepe LePew sugar and creamer. *From the collection of Harvey Linn.* Set, $50-60.

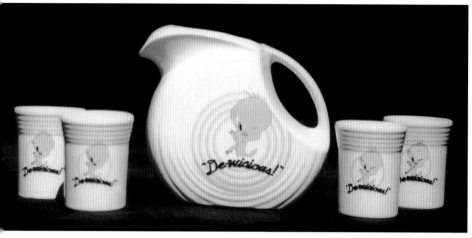

Tweety Bird 60th anniversary disk pitcher set. *Photo courtesy of Tim Maleck.* $75-100.

Tweety and Sylvester Christmas teapot and matching Christmas mugs. *Photo courtesy of Ellie Rovella.* Teapot, $50-60. Mug, $25-30.

Daffy Duck cup and saucer, Sylvester cup and saucer, and Tweety jumbo mug. *From the collection of Harvey Linn.* Cup and saucer sets, $20-25. Jumbo mug, $10-15.

Bugs Bunny sauceboat. *From the collection Harvey Linn.* $25-35.

Scooby-Doo large disk pitcher. *Photo courtesy of Gary Schreiner. From the collection of Jeryl and Gary Schreiner.* $35-45.

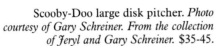

Scooby-Doo mugs, salt and pepper shakers, and 9 inch dinner plate. *Photo courtesy of Gary Schreiner. From the collection of Jeryl and Gary Schreiner.* Mug, white or sea mist green, $10-15. Salt and pepper shakers, $15-23. 9 inch dinner plate, $22-27. Teacup and saucer set (saucer not pictured), $20-25.

Bugs Bunny, Sylvester, Porky Pig, and Daffy Duck 9 inch rim soup bowls. $15-25. Bugs Bunny and Porky Pig teacup and saucer sets. $20-25. *From the collection of Harvey Linn.*

Daffy Duck, Tweety Bird, Sylvester, Bugs Bunny, and Porky Pig mugs. *From the collection of Harvey Linn.* $10-15.

Tweety Bird teapot. *From the collection of Harvey Linn.* $45-55.

Collector Club Exclusives

Due to the growing popularity of Fiesta, The Fiesta Club of America (FCoA) and the Homer Laughlin China Collectors Association (IILCCA) were formed. The FCoA was short-lived and is no longer in existence; but, while it was operating it offered its members a set of collector Fiesta serving trays. In 1995, the FCoA offered the first in its series, a lilac tray. Approximately 300 of these trays were made and are considered by many as the rarest lilac item known to exist. Other trays followed: persimmon in 1996; sapphire in 1997; chartreuse, and black in 1998; and pearl gray in 1999.

The HLCCA was formed in 1998 and is still in existence today. The association began to produce a series of juice pitchers in 1999 that depicted important events taking place throughout the 1930s. In 1999 the first of its juice pitcher series was offered to its members, the 1930 pearl gray juice disk pitcher featuring the Chrysler Building. Only 350 of these pitchers were offered for sale to HLCCA members. Other pitchers followed: 1999, the 1931 white Dick Tracy pitcher; 2000, the 1932 yellow radio disk pitcher; and in 2001, the black 1933 Chicago Worlds Fair pitcher. Five hundred Dick Tracy pitchers, four hundred radio pitchers, and five hundred Chicago World's Fair pitchers were made available to HLCCA members. During the HLCCA's 1999 conference, a large white Dick Tracy disk pitcher, a sample piece, was auctioned off to raise funds for the organization. In 2001, two juniper 1933 Chicago World Fair juice pitchers, also samples, were auctioned off to raise money for the HLCCA.

The HLCCA also commissioned HLC to produce awards for its yearly convention for members participating in competitions. The awards include the grand award, the gold award, the silver award, the bronze award, and the Jonathan Parry award. The grand award is a cobalt blue presentation bowl with a decal signature of Jonathan Parry, the gold award is a cobalt blue disk pitcher with a decal signature of Fredrick Rhead, the silver award is a pearl gray juice disk pitcher with a Fredrick Rhead decal signature, and the bronze is a white mini disk pitcher with the Fredrick Rhead decal signature. These awards are given for displays presented at the HLCCA conventions. The Jonathan Parry award is a pearl gray millennium III vase decorated with the decal signature of Parry. It is awarded to the author submitting the best article of the year that appears in the HLCCA's magazine, *The Dish*.

Lilac FCoA tray. *From the collection of Harvey Linn.* $200-300.

Sapphire FCoA tray, $40-60.

HLCCA juice disk pitcher series: 1930 Chrysler Building pitcher in pearl gray, $225-300. 1931 Dick Tracy pitcher in white, $80-100. 1932 Radio pitcher in yellow, $45-50. 1933 World's Fair disk pitcher in black, $55-65. A large white Dick Tracy disk pitcher sold at auction in 1999 for $1,000.

Two juniper World's Fair juice disk pitchers sold at auction for $900 and $1,200 in 2001.

The HLCCA gold and silver awards. NEV.

The Jonathan Parry award. *Photo courtesy of Mark Gonzalez.* NEV.

Millennium Disk Pitchers, Beverage Sets, and Millennium Plate

As the nation prepared to celebrate the new millennium, HLC provided collectors with many items to commemorate the event. Bloomingdale's pearl beverage set, consisting of a pearl gray disk pitcher and four tumblers, was a popular choice among many post 86 collectors. The pitcher is decorated with thirteen stars representing Fiesta's thirteen colors. One of the four tumblers in the set was decorated with a lilac number two on its side while the three remaining tumblers are decorated with zeros on their sides, one in lilac, cobalt blue, and chartreuse. In 2001, Bloomingdale's again offered its customers a persimmon disk pitcher with matching tumblers.

Macy's millennium item was a commemorative plate. The white plate sported a dancing girl swirling around in a party dress while holding a champagne glass and came in two versions; one with the words "The New Millennium" printed in chartreuse and blue letters, and the second version with the word Millennium printed in blue letters.

To celebrate the new millennium, HLC produced several decal disk pitchers for department stores. One of the memorable disk pitchers was made for Sterns department stores. The drawing on the decal, done by Judi Noble, was of the New York skyline. Included in the drawing were the Trade Center Towers that were destroyed by terrorists on September 11, 2001.

Made as an exclusive for Sterns Department Stores, this large disk pitcher was made to commemorate the new millennium. White pitcher, $80-100. Pearl gray pitcher (pictured), $60-80. Yellow pitcher, $50-60.

2000 disk pitcher beverage set made exclusively for Bloomingdale's. *From the collection of Harvey Linn.* CRV.

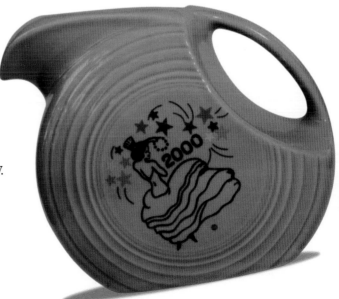

2001 disk pitcher beverage set made exclusively for Bloomingdale's. CRV.

Macy's exclusive millennium plate. *Photo courtesy of Ellie Rovella.* $10-15.

Millennium large disk pitcher shown in chartreuse, cobalt blue, pearl gray, and yellow. *From the collection of Harvey Linn.* $25-35.

60th Anniversary Decal Ware

In 1998, HLC released a series of items to celebrate the 60th anniversary of Fiesta. Some of the more popular items released were the beverage sets. According to factory records, the HLC art department started developing the beverage sets in June of 1995. The beverage sets were produced in sapphire, lilac, turquoise, cobalt blue, periwinkle blue, persimmon, and rose. Although exact figures are not available, it has been estimated that only 300 rose beverage sets were made, making them extremely hard to find. Some collectors and dealers were upset when they saw HLC released sapphire and lilac beverage sets since those two colors had been discontinued from the general Fiesta line. They feared that HLC was going back on its word to discontinue those colors and that prices for sapphire and lilac items would fall. There are no exact figures available as to how many of these sets were made, but the sapphire sets were limited to only 180 days. In addition to the beverage sets, HLC also released 60th anniversary mugs and round serving trays.

60th anniversary beverage set shown in lilac and sapphire blue. Lilac set, $75-125. Sapphire set, $60-75.

60th anniversary mug in persimmon. $10-12.

94

Exclusive Decal Ware

One of the easiest and least expensive ways to customize dinnerware is to add an exclusive decal to an existing piece. In 2001, HLC released the Fiesta Watercolor Series. An exclusive of Bloomingdale's, the series consisted of a round serving tray, a mug, and four 9 inch luncheon plates. Decorated with a persimmon, olive, grape, or garden decal, they were not popular with collectors or the general public and the series was quickly discontinued.

In 2001, HLC produced the "Diner" mug and 9 inch plate for Macy's West. By adding the "Diner" decal to white Fiesta already had in stock, Macy's was able to offer their customers an affordable and exclusive Fiesta series. Reminiscent of Macy's Quatra line, the "Diner" set is a fun addition to any post 86 collection.

In 1999, J.C. Penney's jumped on the exclusive decal ware bandwagon and introduced their "Dancing Lady" beverage set. The set, introduced in chartreuse, was made in yellow in 2000 and pearl gray in 2001.

Post 86 "Watercolor" tray. *From the collection of Gary and Jeryl Schreiner.* $35-40.

Post 86 "Watercolor" mug. *From the collection of Gary and Jeryl Schreiner.* $20-25.

Post 86 "Watercolor" plates. $18-20.

Diner mug, CRV.

Dancing Lady disk pitcher beverage set, shown in chartreuse and yellow, made exclusively for J.C. Penney's. *From the collection of Harvey Linn.* Chartreuse and yellow set, $50-75. Gray set (not shown), CRV.

Fiesta Signature Plate and Collector Plate

The 11 3/4 inch Fiesta signature plate, or dealer plate, is a promotional piece for stores that carry the Fiesta line. Signature plates are commonly used as an advertising tool; but, with the popularity of Fiesta, they are also popular collector pieces. Usually found in white, they are also found in apricot and yellow. When a curator at the Smithsonian's American History Museum contacted HLC, asking for a sample of their post 86 Fiesta for the museum's collection, HLC sent a white signature plate. Similar to the signature plate, HLC also produced a 10 inch collector's plate. It is a Betty Crocker exclusive, although it can also be found at the HLC outlet store.

Fiesta signature plate. Most often found in white, this dealer plate is also made in apricot and yellow. White plate, $20-25. Apricot and yellow plate, $50-70.

The collector plate was offered through the Betty Crocker catalog and at the HLC outlet store. CRV.

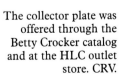

96

Promotional Decal Ware

In past years, many companies have advertised by placing their logo on HLC productions and today's companies are no exception. From local radio stations to Walt Disney, companies use decal ware to promote their companies or services by creating an inexpensive premium to give away to their customers and employees. One of the most well known and sought after promotional wares is the Mickey Mouse disk pitcher. Approximately 2088 pitchers were made for the Disney Channel as an incentive for its employees and are highly prized on the secondary market.

An advertising mug for Tamarack, located in Beckley, West Virginia. CRV.

Mickey Mouse disk pitcher. $200-300.

9 inch advertising plate made for a local radio station located in Weirton, West Virginia. $10-12.

Seasonal Fiesta

HLC started to market seasonal Fiesta late in 1999. The first offering was a "Happy Pumpkin" series. The ware was made with persimmon Fiesta and had small black decal that changed the ceramic surface of the item into the carved face of a Halloween pumpkin. Advertised on the HLC web page and sold through the HLC outlet store, they were moderately popular with collectors.

The next seasonal Fiesta offered through the HLC outlet store was the "Triple Hearts for Valentines" series in early 2000. The cinnabar wares had a silver triple heart decal added, making them something a hostess could use at a valentine party. Individual pieces like the bud vase, bread tray, deep dish pie baker, and round serving tray could also be used when giving a loved one flowers and cookies as gifts. This series was also moderately popular with collectors. Released quickly thereafter was the "Shamrock" series on sea mist green. It, too, was available at the HLC outlet store.

By the time the next seasonal Fiesta series was released, "Easter Eggs" in yellow, collectors were growing weary of so many decal items being released for the holidays. Some comments on the web boards included things like, "What next — Ground Hog Day?" Others still thought these series were nice additions to their collections. Adding decals to stock already present in its inventory was an easy and relatively inexpensive way for HLC to create a new product. Without the creative force of Jonathan Parry in its art department, HLC seemingly was scrambling for new ideas to satisfy its customers. Judi Noble's forte has always been her ability to create and produce imaginative decals; so, as art director, she began doing what she does best — creating the seasonal Fiesta line.

The next seasonal Fiesta line, "Mardi Gras," was different from the other seasonal lines. Instead of using cute little decal pictures to decorate its wares, HLC decorated its "Mardi Gras" series by adding stripes to white Fiesta. The green, purple, and gold stripes represent the three traditional colors of the festival. It, too, was available through the outlet.

The final seasonal Fiesta was for the Fourth of July. Two decal series were offered to HLC customers, "Fireworks" and the "Stars and Stripes." The "Fireworks" de-

cal, in blue and rust red, shows stars intertwined in a fireworks display and the "Stars and Stripes" decal, also in blue and rust rcd, depicts the American flag among stars and fireworks. Another decal retail outlet exclusive that matched the "Fireworks" and "Stars and Stripes" series is the "Mom's Apple Pie" 10 inch deep-dish pie baker. Found under the heading "special occasions" on the HLC web board at the outlet store and sold as a Mother's Day item, the pie baker was also a very popular item for any patriotic celebration.

At the time of this writing, HLC announced its next lines of seasonal Fiesta, "Turkey Day" and "Sugar Plum Fairy," would be released soon.

Available items in each of the seasonal Fiesta series

Happy Pumpkin series	Mardi Gras
Fiesta mug	Sold as a set with dinner and salad
plate, 6 7/8 inch	
10 inch pie baker	Bowl and mug
Round candleholder	
S & P shaker	
Pizza plate	

The Shamrock, Triple Hearts, Easter Egg, Fireworks, and Stars and Stripes series come in the following items:

Bread tray	Deep dish pie baker
Cup	Mug
Dinner plate 10 1/2 inch	Two cup teapot
Round serving tray	Bud vase
Saucer (undecorated)	

Turkey Day Series

Bread tray	Pizza tray
Cup	Deep dish pie baker
Dinner plate 10 1/2 inch	Mug
Round serving tray	Candle stick holder
Saucer (undecorated)	

Sugar Plum Fairy Series

Round candle holder	Dinner plate
Cup	Oval platter
Saucer	Sauceboat
Bread tray	

"Mom's Apple Pie" deep dish pie baker. CRV.

"Triple Hearts" 10 inch dinner plate. *Photo courtesy of Gary Schreiner. From the collection of Jeryl and Gary Schreiner.* CRV.

"Easter Egg," "Happy Pumpkin," and Christmas mugs sold at the HLC outlet store. *Photo courtesy of Gary Schreiner. From the collection of Jeryl and Gary Schreiner.* CRV.

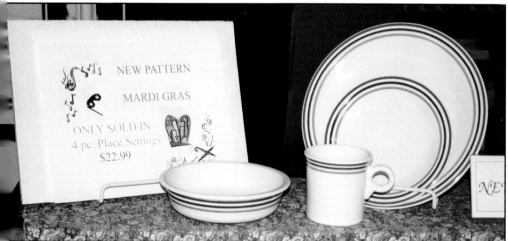

"Mardi Gras" four piece place setting at the HLC outlet store. CRV.

"Shamrock" bud vase. CRV.

"Stars and Stripes" and "Fireworks" mugs sold at the HLC outlet store. *Photo courtesy of Gary Schreiner. From the collection of Jeryl and Gary Schreiner.* CRV.

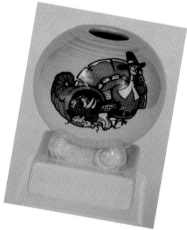

"Happy Thanksgiving" bulb candle holder. CRV.

"Sugar Plum Fairy" cup and saucer. CRV.

Mega China

In 1998, Joe Solito and Sam Collings approached HLC about creating a new line of dinnerware for their company, Mega China. Solito says he and his partner have always admired the Fiesta line of dinnerware and wanted to do business with HLC because they were impressed with the quality of all their products. After discussing their plans with Dave Conley, the two men met with the Jonathan Parry and other members of the HLC art department. Collings brought several decal design ideas with him to their meetings. Most of his original design ideas were deemed too impractical or too expensive to produce. Working with Judi Noble, Solito and Collings have created four pattern designs: Champagne, Midnight, Mystique, and Moonshine.

Since its introduction, "My First Fiesta" has been very popular among many Fiesta collectors; but, what do you do if you need additional cups and saucers for those extra guests that might drop in at your next tea party? Mega China answers that question with its line

"Champagne" by Mega China. 10 inch dinner plate and mug. CRV.

"Mystique" by Mega China. 10 inch dinner plate and 19 ounce bowl. CRV.

"Moonshine" by Mega China. 10 inch dinner plate and mug. CRV.

of Fiesta glazed teacups and saucers that match those found in the "My First Fiesta" tea set. Offered in cinnabar, cobalt blue, juniper, pearl gray, periwinkle, persimmon, rose, sea mist green, sunflower yellow, turquoise, white, and yellow, these cute items make an excellent addition to the basic tea set and can be bought online at www.megachina.com.

Chapter 5

Fiesta go alongs

Postcard brochure HLC included with each place setting of Fiesta tableware. The photograph in the pink picture frame is of Parker Parry. Jonathan liked the picture so much, he wanted to use it in the advertisement for the go alongs. *Courtesy of The Homer Laughlin China Company.*

Official licensees of The Homer Laughlin China Company. *Courtesy of The Homer Laughlin China Company.*

The marketing of Fiesta go alongs has been going along for quite some time. To promote sales during lean economic times, tableware makers, in association with HLC, have offered glassware, tablecloths, and other kitchen items that complemented Fiesta's bright colors and promoted Fiesta sales. The marketing strategy behind the contemporary post 86 go alongs is similar in that as the ceramic tableware market grew in the late 1990s, tableware producers placed a renewed focus on the "total tableware" concept, the marketing strategy similar to that which had helped promote the sales of Fiesta during more difficult economic periods.

In 1997, casual dinnerware sales accounted for 75.5% of all ceramic tableware sold in the United States. During the same time, glassware sales also rose. While major pottery companies such as HLC continued to create new lines, they also started placing emphasis on the design of new glassware and other products that complemented their tableware.

Working with the art department at HLC, Moderme Glass Co., of Aliquippa, Pennsylvania, decorates glass stemware and tumblers that match post 86 Fiesta tableware. In an article published by the Society of Glass and Ceramic Decorators, Tom McKnight, president of Moderme said that although the glassware is decorated and packaged for sale at his plant, it is distributed solely by HLC's marketing network.

HLC licensed fifteen companies to produce everything from juicers to silverware with the goal of developing further market share through the promotion of Fiesta go alongs and its own Fiesta tableware. In an interview published in the *Pittsburgh Post Gazette*, March 17, 1999, Jonathan discussed how he and others at HLC developed the new line of Fiesta go alongs and his vision for all the new products. He stated, "The idea was not to copy Fiesta, but to incorporate the Fiesta concept into the new product's identity. When you just copy, it isn't innovative.

We wanted a look and something that would be part of the total package." In an interview with *HFN*, a weekly newspaper of home products retailing, Dave Conley added, "The department stores are always looking for new things. Our new licensee products keep the pressure off us by offering new products in different categories and build a greater awareness of the Fiesta brand."

Perfect as gifts for the new bride or to create a themed look in a kitchen, the new go alongs were named "Genuine Fiesta Accessories." Since no store carried all the Genuine Fiesta Accessories, and to generate interest in the entire line of go alongs, IILC included a full color brochure with each place setting of Fiesta tableware with photos and information about the line. Some go along items were short lived, some were not, and some have a story all their own.

A variety of Fiesta go alongs on display at the HLC factory showroom.

The Mighty OJ Juicer and the Metrokane Ice Crusher

Of all the post 86 Fiesta go alongs, the Mighty OJ manual juicer, with its classic retro design, stands above the rest. Designed by Espartaco Ramirez in the 1930s and manufactured by Metrokane of New York, the juicer's design won it a spot in the Museum of Modern Art in 1984. A friend of Ricki Kane's, Metrokane's founder, first thought of the idea of using the juicer as a Fiesta go along. Ricki, her husband, and Bob Laimer, Metrokane's marketing director, all agreed that the juicer would indeed fit nicely into HLC's go along program because both Fiesta and the Mighty OJ Juicer had been designed and developed during the '30s. After consulting with HLC about using the Mighty OJ Juicer as a Fiesta go along, it was decided that Metrokane's Ice Crusher (which had also been designed by Ramirez) would also make a nice go along. No longer produced in the Fiesta colors, the Mighty OJ manual juicer and the ice crusher are still available in the company's standard colors and remain successful in the marketplace.

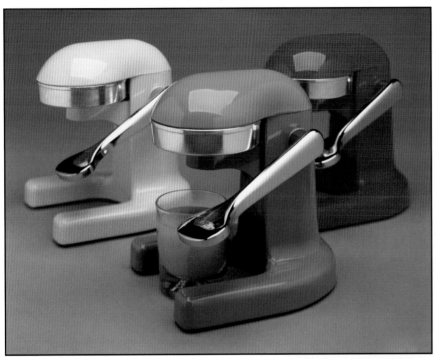

The Mighty OJ and the Mighty Ice Crusher by Metrokane. *Photos courtesy of Bob Larimer.*

Fiesta Flatware

In the early 1990s, the post 86 Fiesta dinnerware line had made a major impact in the marketplace. Banking on its popularity, HLC embarked on a new Fiesta project — designing its own line of flatware.

It is unclear who came up with the idea first. The sales department, headed by Dave Conley, and the art department work very closely together on the development of all the Fiesta go alongs. The first Fiesta flatware was designed by Jonathan. An HLC press release described the flatware as follows: "The Homer Laughlin China Company now offers colored-handle stainless steel flatware to complement its Fiesta dinnerware. Originally released during the depression, Fiesta is the most popular dinnerware sold in the United States. The flatware will complement the art deco styling of Fiesta, and is available in all the nine colors; white, black, rose, apricot, cobalt blue, yellow, turquoise, periwinkle blue, and sea mist green. The colored handles are sculpted with two flowing lines that create a mirror image on either side of the stainless body. The fastening is done without rivets for a clean, more formal look. The place setting will consist of one each, soup spoon, dessert spoon, salad fork, dinner fork, and butter knife. Completer service pieces are also part of the line. The place settings will be sold in single boxes by color, allowing the consumer to choose multi-colored dinnerware and coordinating flatware."

After the designs were completed, HLC selected Michael Lloyd Associates, Inc. of Oceanside, New York, to act as its agent in the development of the new flatware product line. The agent selected the manufacturer, assisted and advised in the development of the product line, negotiated with the manufacturer on HLC's behalf, and conducted quality inspections during the product development and prior to acceptance of the finished product. Blueprints for the new flatware were drawn up in September of 1991 and shortly thereafter Stanley Roberts Inc. of Lodi, New Jersey, was chosen as the product's manufacturer.

As the Fiesta dinnerware color line expanded, so did the colors offered by Stanley Roberts. At the time of this writing, Fiesta flatware is offered in white, rose, cobalt blue, yellow, turquoise, periwinkle blue, sea mist green, persimmon, chartreuse, gray, juniper, and sunflower.

Apricot and lilac had been discontinued, but in September of 2001 Stanley Roberts announced the impending release of sapphire and the reissuing of lilac. The Christmas Fiesta flatware was made in bright red and emerald green and came in a special white tin box featuring the Fiesta Dancing Lady. The Christmas flatware was discontinued in 1999.

Since the flatware's introduction, the line has expanded to include other styles of Fiesta flatware. They include a fifteen piece and a seven piece cutlery set, four patterns of stainless steel flatware (minus the plastic handles), and the Cycles pattern of Fiesta flatware.

Fiesta flatware shown in lilac. *Photo courtesy of Ellie Rovella.*

Chapter 6

Fiesta Mates

Fiesta Mates are HLC restaurant ware items dipped in Fiesta colors and offered for sale to HLC's foodservice clientele. Once considered strictly Fiesta Mates, the sugar caddy, jumbo mug, saucer, and the jumbo bowl (also known as the chili bowl), are now also considered part of the Fiesta line.

A new development in the Fiesta Mates line is the new Colorations line. Eight of the ten colors in the Colorations line are also used in HLC's Fiesta line. The Colorations line is distinctive for incorporating geometric shapes into the design of the bowls. At the time of this writing, these bowls come in the following shapes: stars, squares, and triangles.

Other Fiesta Mates include the 10" baker, the bouillon cup, the A.D. cup and saucer, the jumbo pasta bowl, the Denver mug, the river mug, the jumbo cup and saucer, the Seville ramekin, the skillet, the Irish coffee mug, the tower mug, the small creamer, the colonial teapot, the 18 oz. chili bowl, and the handleless 13 oz. soup mug.

A Fiesta Mate that raised a lot of eyebrows was the Red Lobster saucer (a small bowl made primarily as restaurant ware) dubbed, "The Red Lobster Bowl." This bowl was made for Red Lobster Restaurants and had a glaze very similar to sapphire. The glaze was a special 60/40 cobalt blue/ clear glaze which many people mistook for the discontinued sapphire glaze.

On November 2, 2001, HLC announced on its web page that the Seville ramekin, the river mug, the Irish coffee mug, the skillet, and the A.D. cup and saucer were no longer available in Fiesta colors.

There are two pottery marks used on the Fiesta Mates line: a stamp mark and a molded mark.

Jumbo mugs in periwinkle blue and rose. CRV.

Jumbo mugs with decal applications.
From the collection of Harvey Linn.
CRV.

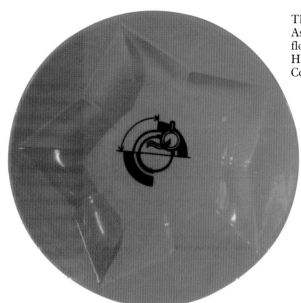

The logo of the Homer Laughlin China Collectors Club Association decorates this star bowl produced in sunflower. The bowl was given to the guests attending the HLCCA's 2001 convention. The star bowl is part of HLC's Coloration line. NEV.

HLC Fiesta Mate skillet shown in cinnabar. CRV.

Denver mug shown in rose and persimmon. The square persimmon bowl is from HLC's Coloration line. CRV.

This multi-ringed plate, resembling sapphire blue, was supposedly made for and rejected by a restaurant chain and sold through the HLC outlet store. They can also be found in turquoise, sea mist green, and persimmon. *From the collection of Harvey Linn.* $15-20.

The Lilac Denver mug, sitting next to a post 86 lilac mug, was purchased at the HLC outlet store. Only a few batches of the lilac Denver mugs were made. NEV.

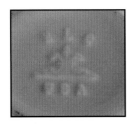

Raised pottery mark found on Fiesta Mates.

The general HLC backstamp use on Fiesta Mates.

Chapter 7

Prototypes, Test Pieces, and Sample Fiesta Items

Unique Shapes and Color Combinations: Where Do They Come From?

A hostess bowl next to the pedestal candle holder that never went into production. When production problems curtailed the release of the candle holder, Jonathan changed its design and created the hostess bowl. Hostess bowl, CRV. Pedestal candle holder, NEV.

Nothing is so intriguing to a Fiesta collector as coming across a rogue Fiesta item. A rogue item is one that was never officially produced, and usually ends up in the secondary market. There are several ways this can happen. Some are legitimate, others less so. I can put to rest the rumors suggesting that some pieces sprout legs and walk out the back door of the factory. There is simply no evidence that evolution plays a part in disappearances at the factory; however, on occasion, members of the HLC management team have given these special items to HLC clients, family members, and friends. And, from time to time, a few of these items have made their way to the secondary market.

Jonathan Parry, well known for his generosity, once gave a prototype pedestal candle holder to a Bloomingdale's executive. This piece was later converted into a hostess bowl. And Parker, Jonathan's son, recalls the time he gave a test cappuccino mug to one of his favorite school teachers. Jonathan also gave many prototypes to friends and family members.

Much has been said about the notorious lilac carafes on HLC collector boards. How did they get out of the factory? No one really knows for certain but with all the brouhaha every time an HLC official sees one for sale, they may indeed have been stolen from the factory. Regardless of their ultimate destination, it is obvious not all rogue pieces that leave the factory are taken illegally. These rarities have no established value but are highly prized by their owners.

How Are Prototypes, Test Pieces, and Samples Different?

When the HLC art department introduces a new product idea, a series of steps are taken before the finished product is ready for the marketplace. After management approves a new product idea, the modeler creates a clay model of the designer's concept. This model, called the mold master, is used to make plaster molds which are used in the ceramic production process. A prototype is the original or model after which anything similar in nature is formed. Using the mold master, a mold of the new design is created and a prototype is produced. Jonathan was known to have signed and dated many of these prototypes. He did so in order to document the history of the particular piece. These items are very rare and special finds.

After a prototype is made and approved by management or an HLC client, the art department begins to make test pieces. Test pieces are generally made in batches of twelve and are used to determine the development of any problems that might occur when a new design is fired. For example, many of the Bloomingdale's pedestal candle stand test pieces cracked when they were fired in the kiln. After a few minor changes were performed on the design, the problem persisted and the pedestal candle stand was scrapped. Through running of test pieces, HLC solves potential problems by correcting the defects in a products design before it goes into large scale production.

Test pieces are also produced when HLC develops a new glaze. For example, sapphire was developed when Bloomingdale's wanted to sell Fiesta in its own exclusive color. After the glaze was developed by the art department and chosen by Bloomingdale's, numerous items of greenware, randomly taken off the production line, were fired as test pieces using the newly developed sapphire glaze. As with all test items, the art department was looking for any potential production problems. A number of these items were shown to the buyers from Bloomingdale's who made their final selection of what sapphire pieces they would offer to their customers. Parker Parry recalls that Jonathan, in his capacity as art director, had taken many of these sapphire test pieces home with him. When Bloomingdale's made its final selection, these test pieces, including a very rare sapphire coffee server, nearly made their way to a local flea market because, "they were cluttering up the place." On Parker's insistence, the sapphire test pieces were saved and stored in their attic.

Numerous rogue sapphire items have made their way into the secondary market and some, like the salt and pepper shakers, have been found with boxes marked "sapphire." It's possible that Bloomingdale's may have ordered the salt and pepper shakers and later changed its mind about taking them. It is impossible to know how many rogue sapphire items there are, but they are prized additions to any post 86 Fiesta collection.

The lilac carafes that have created such a scandal in the secondary market are also test pieces. The art department was developing the post 86 Fiesta carafe about the time lilac was going out of production and when it came time to fire a test batch, they used lilac glaze. By the time the carafe was introduced into the marketplace, lilac had been discontinued. And, unfortunately for collectors, a lilac carafe was never mass produced.

Sample items are less controversial as rogue items than either prototypes or test pieces. Pleasing the customer is what good marketing is all about and at HLC they strive to do just that. When a customer comes to HLC with a product idea, the sales department, as well as the art department, work with the customer to meet the customer's needs. One way they do this is by producing sample items. Samples are previews that allow a customer to make changes in an item's appearance. Many times decals are used to customize wares for a customer's specific needs. An example of this would be a restaurant ordering customized decal ware featuring its name and logo. Other times, customers interested in selling an exclusive item are offered the option of adding a decal to a stock item as an economical way of making an exclusive item for sale. A popular example of this is the exclusive Fiesta line sold at the American Museum of Natural History featuring retro space decals. Since the colored glaze will show through a decal after it is fired distorting the decal's original colors, samples allow the customer to see how the decal will look on the finished product. If the customers do not like what they see, the colors in the decal can be modified and another sample made. Some sample items that never went into production have made it into the secondary market, fetching hefty prices.

Although rogue Fiesta items make nice additions to any collection, collectors should certainly be especially careful not to purchase any items which have been stolen from HLC. Therefore, buying from reputable dealers is always the best policy.

The rose cappuccino mug, a test piece, has a thicker wall than the cappuccino mug that was eventually released, shown in sunflower. The test mug is heavier and more awkward to hold. Sunflower cappuccino mug, CRV. Rose cappuccino mug test piece, NEV.

The first Fiesta deep dish pie baker made. Sign and dated by Jonathan Parry. NEV.

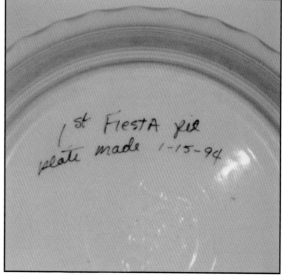

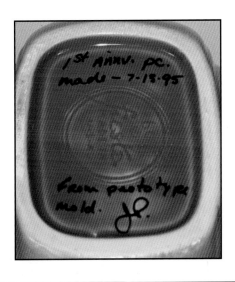

A prototype post 86 disk pitcher made from a vintage prototype mold. Signed and dated by Jonathan Parry.

The first mini disk pitcher made. Signed
and dated by Jonathan Parry. NEV.

Trivet prototype in periwinkle blue. Sign
and dated by Jonathan Parry.

Prototypes are not limited to pottery. This holiday
Fiesta flatware box is a prototype. Its storage box is
signed and dated by Jonathan Parry.

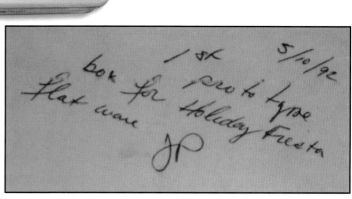

With the rise in popularity of post 86 Fiesta, reports of counterfeit autographs placed on Fiesta items are circulating within the collecting community. Collectors need to familiarize themselves with the signatures of Jonathan Parry, Judi Noble, and Joseph Geisse. Examples and Jonathan's signature are shown throughout this chapter. Pictured is Judi Noble's signature and the initials and signature of Joseph Geisse. These items were signed by Judi and Joseph in my presence and are in my personal collection.

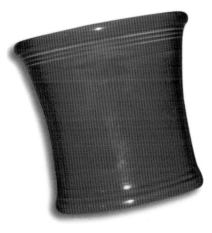

Post 86 Fiesta ice bucket test piece. At this time, the ice bucket is not in production. NEV.

One of four test trivets.
Signed by Jonathan Parry.

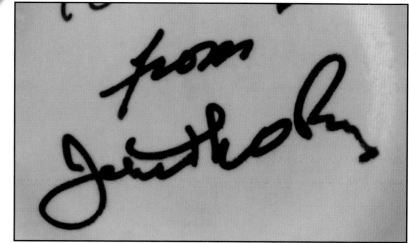

Sapphire blue coffeepot from
Jonathan Parry's collection.
NEV.

Sapphire blue sauceboat from
Jonathan Parry's collection. NEV.

Sapphire blue sugar bowl from Jonathan
Parry's collection. NEV.

Sapphire blue mini disk pitcher from Jonathan
Parry's collection. NEV.

Pair of sapphire blue pyramid candle holders
from Jonathan Parry's collection. NEV.

Sapphirc blue individual sugar and creamer from Jonathan Parry's collection. NEV.

Set of sapphire blue napkin rings from Jonathan Parry's collection. NEV.

Pair of sapphire blue round candle holders from Jonathan Parry's collection. NEV.

Sapphire blue bud vase from Jonathan Parry's collection. NEV.

Sapphire blue juice disk pitcher from Jonathan Parry's collection. NEV.

Jonathan often brought his work home with him, including these test pieces that were displayed in his family room during one of my visits. He graciously allowed me to photograph this 8 inch chartreuse vase and pyramid candle stick holder fired in a matted glaze. NEV.

Before the raspberry presentation bowls were fired, the glaze was tested. This is one of those test pieces. It is a post 86 lidded raspberry casserole. NEV.

Individual sugar and creamer test pieces. *Photo by Mark Burnett. From the collection of Mark and Cathy Burnett.* NEV.

This lilac glaze test piece was made using a 9 1/2 inch platter that was discontinued in 1990 when a restyled version was introduced. This piece is sign and dated by Jonathan Parry. NEV.

Sugar bowl from a sugar and creamer set. This test piece was fired in two different colored glazes, avocado green and black. NEV.

Looking more like teal than juniper, Jonathan made this presentation bowl in the HLC art department shortly before his death. NEV.

119

7 inch black 60th anniversary plate never made for the retail market. NEV.

Like the Watercolor series made for Bloomingdale's, this sample set was slated to go into production for Linens and Things. This series is called Seasons of Fiesta. The set never went into production. NEV.

More of a promotional piece than a sample, this pearl gray Fiesta 2000 charger was to be used at houseware shows to promote HLC's new line of dinnerware. It's said that Jonathan came up with the slogan on the plate. Only four of these plates are known to exist. NEV.

Members of the art department wanted to commemorate the new millennium in a very special way by creating this decorative decal bearing Jonathan's name. Jonathan was touched but sidelined the design. NEV.

Samples of the HLCCA 1933 World's Fair juice disk pitcher. Shown in black, sunflower, cinnabar, cobalt blue, yellow, sea mist green, chartreuse, and juniper. Juniper, $900-1,200. Standard black pitcher, $55-65. Other pitchers, NEV.

This is a sample cup for the "Some Bunny's Been Eating Out of My Fiesta" children's set. The decal on the outside is fired on while the decal inside the cup is added later. It is not fired into the cup. NEV.

Sample mug that never went into production. *Photo by Mark Burnett. From the collection of Mark and Cathy Burnett.*

A sample sauceboat made for Warner Brothers. It never went into production. NEV.

This very odd sample demitasse cup was made for Walt Disney. Using the demitasse cup body from their restaurant line, the HLC art department added a handle resembling an ear. The sample is shown next to a post 86 Fiesta demitasse cup and saucer in apricot. Disney rejected the idea. NEV.

Hawaiiana Ware samples. Although Jonathan asked Macy's if Lynn Blocker Krantz could use their exclusive millennium II base for her Hawaiiana Ware collection, Macy's declined his request. The Fiesta Hawaiiana Ware dish set was never released. The disk pitcher and mug are presently the only Fiesta items in the Hawaiiana Ware line. NEV.

A sample baseball sugar bowl. NEV.

Some unique items are not made by HLC. A decal, purchased from a decal company not far from the HLC factory, was fired onto a post 86 cobalt blue bud vase by a Fiesta collector. NEV.

Some unique pieces are not test items or samples piece, they are manufacturing flukes. A Fiesta collector found this apricot presentation bowl at the HLC outlet store. The collector bought several bowls out of a stack ranging from a deep apricot with a tiny, almost unnoticeable tint of rose under the foot, to almost all rose with a slight tint of apricot. Apparently these were sprayed when factory workers were changing the glaze in the equipment from apricot to rose. NEV.

If a collector is lucky, a unique piece, like this small Fiesta styled compote, can be found at the HLC outlet store. The compote was made for a restaurant customer. HLC never introduced the compote into their retail Fiesta line.

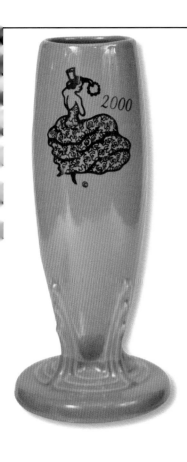

Where did these "mystery" dancing lady pieces come from and who were they made for? Some believe they may have been made for a charity benefit but no one I contacted really seemed to know.

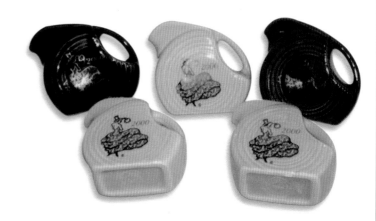

Chapter 8

China Specialties

In 1985, Virginia Lee, a long time antique dealer and Fiesta collector, and her son, Joel Wilson, contacted HLC to produce a commemorative piece celebrating Fiesta's 50th anniversary.

Virginia and Joel expanded upon their initial idea, and further pieces were produced. From this arrangement China Specialties was born.

In 1986, before post 86 Fiesta was introduced into the general marketplace, a 10-set collection of commemorative mugs was offered through China Specialties. Each of the ten white mugs in a set was decorated with the Fiesta Dancing Senorita Trademark in one of the vintage Fiesta colors: red, yellow, turquoise, medium green, light green, forest green, cobalt, rose, chartreuse, and gray. HLC produced the mugs by using a Fiesta-like handle from its York mug, which is a shape found in its restaurant china line. Five hundred eighty three sets were produced and offered to the public at $149 each.

China Specialties capitalized upon the popularity of their products by expanding their mail order business to include retail space, thus becoming one of the first businesses in the East Liverpool Antique Mall (East Liverpool, Ohio), where they are still located. Joel, a practical businessman, had a lot of stock in storage. Many of the items were flawed, not by factory standards (like pin holes or skips in the glaze), but by the standards of the collecting community. By opening up his store, he required less warehouse space, and he used his new outlet to sell his wares to customers that wouldn't find those types of flaws objectionable. Other merchants joined Joel, opening businesses in what has become one of the most popular antique shopping malls in the area.

When asked why China Specialties' items are so successful, Joel responds, "By introducing historical elements, we have items that could have been designed back in the 1930s. It's getting harder to find good quality vintage items at any price in the marketplace. We offer vintage style at reasonable prices." Joel works with local graphic artists to create the designs and decals for most of their products. China Specialties doesn't sell reproductions, only additional items to existing lines. Each item is clearly marked "China Specialties" and dated on the bottom of each piece. Joel proudly adds, "We do business completely above board. We never misrepresent our products."

Mugs from the 50th anniversary mug set. A complete set of ten, $300. Individual mugs, $30-35.

Decals and Proposition 65

In 1986, Proposition 65, California's Safe Drinking Water and Toxic Enforcement Act made a major impact on America's ceramic industry. It mandated that not only glazes be lead free, but that decorative ceramic items carry warning labels if overglaze decals containing lead and cadmium were used on food contact surfaces. Heavy metals, such as lead and cadmium, can migrate into foods, especially acidic foods such as oranges and tomatoes. The acids in foods can speed dissolution of heavy metals, making food poisonous. China Specialties decals are not applied and fired at HLC and because they use overglaze decals (decals that are fired at a lower temperature and don't sink all the way into the glaze) that contain lead and cadmium, the items are marked in accordance with the law. Some collectors thought the items were marked "for display only" because the decals could easily scratch off and were con-

The vase on the right is decorated with an overglaze decal, the one on the left has an inglaze decal. Note the difference between the red in each decal. The red in the overglaze decal is brighter and more vibrant than the red in the inglaze decal which looks duller and brown in tone. Because overglaze decals are fired at lower temperatures, the colors don't "burn out" like the colors in the inglaze example. *Photo courtesy of Joel Wilson.*

cerned about whether these items could be washed in soap and water. All items can be safely washed and decals will not scratch off. China Specialties decals are, in many ways, like those used on vintage HLC wares including the old Sun Porch, Mexicana, and Virginia Rose. Vintage wares were also decorated with overglaze decals. However, unlike the old decals that aren't dishwasher safe, the new decals are and won't fade or wash off if placed in a dishwasher.

In 1996, to commemorate the 60th anniversary of Fiesta, China Specialties created the Circa 36 disk pitcher. It was only available to subscribers of The Fiesta Collectors' Quarterly. Commissioning a local artist to paint an arrangement of Vintage Fiesta items, Joel turned the image into a ceramic decal that was fired onto a black post 86 Fiesta disk pitcher. The artwork was based on a 1965 HLC Fiesta advertising pamphlet. Each pitcher was backstamped with a date, serial number, and a notation that it was made as an exclusive for the Fiesta Collectors' Quarterly. The buyer also had the option of having his or her name placed on the bottom of the pitcher. The pitcher originally sold for $49.95. In the Winter 1999-2000 edition of *The Fiesta Collectors' Quarterly*, members of the organization were offered a new exclusive, a mini Circa 36 pitcher. A limited edition of 500, each is numbered and backstamped in gold with the words, "FCQ Members Exclusive- Circa 36." Each item also has a serial number but, unlike the first Circa 36 pitcher, isn't dated nor could these smaller pitchers be personalized. Time will tell if these pitchers will be as popular or as collectible as their larger counterparts.

Circa 36 Pitcher

Large "Circa 36" disk pitcher, $250-350. Mini "Circa 36" disk pitcher, $40.

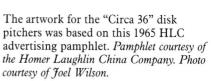

The artwork for the "Circa 36" disk pitchers was based on this 1965 HLC advertising pamphlet. *Pamphlet courtesy of the Homer Laughlin China Company. Photo courtesy of Joel Wilson.*

Moon Over Miami

Moon Over Miami, also introduced in 1996, was a popular limited edition line among many Fiesta collectors. Joel's concept for the Moon Over Miami line was the result of too much black Fiesta in his stock. This overstock was the mother of creativity for the match-up of his black Fiesta with a decal, making a unique item that could be marketed as an exclusive. He found the now famous flamingo decal at a tile company. When the Moon Over Miami line was introduced, many Fiesta collectors immediately flocked to the wares. Joel introduced the Moon Over Miami series in the 1996 fall edition of *The Fiesta Collector's Quarterly*. The first items introduced were the covered casserole, bulb candleholders, the large juice and mini disk pitchers, bud and large vases, sugar and creamer with the tray, a 5 1/2 inch candy bowl, and salt and pepper shakers. Prices for these items when they were introduced ranged from $5.95 to 39.95, and quantities were limited to no more than 500 of each item. In Joel's Winter 1997/98 edition of *The Fiesta Collector's Quarterly*, he introduced the Moon Over Miami Carafe, display sign, and the 1998 calendar plate. The calendar plates were offered in two sizes — nine and ten inches — and only two hundred of each plate were made. The Carafe was also limited to two hundred pieces. Near the end of its production, other Moon Over Miami items, which included a handled serving tray, napkin rings, regular teapot, set of four tumblers, sugar packet holder, A.D. cup and saucer, covered butter dish, sauce boat, serving bowl, twelve inch rimmed soup bowl, coffee pot, presentation bowl, pair of tripod candleholders, Seville (Fiesta Mate) ramekin, and a set of four mugs, were produced. These, too, were limited to 500 of each item or set.

When asked why he never offered buyers a Moon Over Miami clock, round serving tray, pedestal bowl, deep dish pie baker, or range top salt and pepper shakers, Joel replies that HLC never made many of those items in black. And the clock was a special case; a few were produced, but Joel found that the clock faces were very prone to breaking because the hole in the center of the clock face weakened the structure of the plate, making them split when the decals were fired on.

Not all Moon Over Miami pieces were made in black, a small number were also made in turquoise. Nick-named "Noon Over Miami," these items did not make up a separate line and the few turquoise items produced were included in the final count of 500, the limited production number of each MOM item.

Although these items have been out of production for some time, collectors can still buy some Moon Over Miami items from a limited selection offered at Joel's store in the East Liverpool Antique Mall. The Moon Over Miami series remains in demand by many Fiesta collectors.

"Moon over Miami" store sign. NEV.

"Moon Over Miami" 9 inch calendar plate, $50. 10 inch calendar plate, $50.

Handle decal on the turquoise "Moon Over Miami" 2 cup teapot.

Turquoise "Moon Over Miami" 2 cup teapot, $45. Black "Moon Over Miami" large teapot, $70. Turquoise "Moon Over Miami" large teapot, $55.

"Moon Over Miami" 12 inch rim post bowl, $30; 10 inch vase, $120; individual creamer and sugar bowl, $60 for the set; sugar and creamer set on a figure 8 tray, $60.

Turquoise "Moon Over Miami" 10 inch vase, $70; round candle holders (pair), $40; bud vase, $20; tumbler, $15; bouillon cup, $13.

Black "Moon Over Miami" presentation bowl and turquoise "Moon Over Miami" presentation bowl, $65.

"Moon Over Miami" carafe, $80.

"Moon Over Miami" serving bowl, $30.

"Moon Over Miami" large disk pitcher, $120. Juice disk pitcher, $60.

"Moon Over Miami" round handled serving tray, $70.

"Moon Over Miami" sugar caddy, $30; bud vase, $40; salt and pepper shakers, $30; sugar and creamer on a figure 8 tray, $60.

Sunporch

Sunporch items were introduced to collectors in 1998 and were sold at the China Specialties Store at the Pottery City Antique Mall (East Liverpool, Ohio). Each item was made in white, with the exception of some plates and the clocks, and were offered with the Sunporchdecal. Every item in the line was limited to 500 pieces or sets. In addition to the HLC items, canisters, a wood and ceramic tray, china thimble, refrigerator magnet, and rolling pin were also offered sporting the Sunporch decal. Like the vintage Sunporchdecal, the new decal used by China Specialties contains cadmium and lead which are used to make bright orange and yellow colorants in decals. In accordance with Prop. 65, all Sunporchitems are labeled, "for display use only."

Some researchers believe that Fredrick Rhead designed the original Sunporchdecal. The decal was used by HLC on its Kitchen Kraft line starting in the late 1930s. The company commissioned to produce the Sunporchdecal for China Specialties was the same company that was used by HLC. Some of the details on the decal were refined by the company at Joel's request and the original decal printing plates were altered before pro-

duction on the new Sunporchdecals began. Joel said the lines on the tableware in the decal were clarified to bring out more of their detail. This was done to make it more appealing to today's collector. Internet auction web sites like e-Bay fueled its popularity and prices soared. Joel believes that what made this line so successful is its strong Art Deco influence. Today, it remains a highly collectible item.

"Sunporch 10 inch plate, $20. Butter dish, $30.

"Sunporch" casserole, $60.

"Sunporch" A.D. cup and saucer, $30; millennium III vase, $65; mug, $18; pyramid candlestick holders (pair), $100.

"Sunporch" presentation bowl, $50.

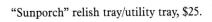

"Sunporch" relish tray/utility tray, $25.

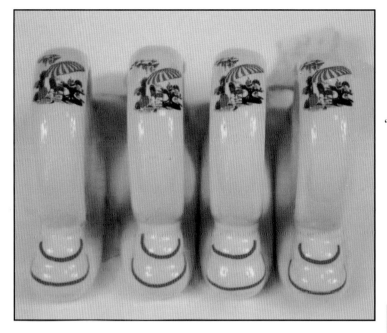

"Sunporch" napkin rings, $15 each.

"Sunporch" large teapot, $65.

"Sunporch" sugar and creamer on a figure 8 tray, $65; 10 inch vase, $90; salt and pepper shakers, $33; spoon rest (made by Hall China), $40.

Fiesta Shelf Display Signs

The Fiesta shelf display signs are popular items among many post 86 Fiesta collectors. Offered as exclusive items by mail to members of the *Fiesta Collectors' Quarterly,* the signs are also available at the East Liverpool Antique Mall. First introduced in the quarterly's winter 96/97 edition, collectors are offered a new color each year: 1996, persimmon; 1997, turquoise and apricot; 1998-1999, chartreuse; 1999, rose; 2000-2001, gray and yellow; 2002, juniper and cinnabar. Decal signs included Moon Over Miami, Sun Porch, and Mexicana. Each color and decal was limited to 500 pieces.

In 1997 HLC mistakenly glazed about 100 signs. Stamped on the bottom as turquoise, in reality they were periwinkle blue. Before the glazes are fired, periwinkle blue and turquoise look very similar. When workers glazed the signs, they mistakenly used the periwinkle blue glaze, thinking it was turquoise. China Specialties accepted the signs and sold them to its customers as especially novel pieces and they are now much sought after. Unlike other China Specialties items that have their decals applied and fired at another location, the sign letters are applied and fired at the HLC plant. The signs are the only items sold by China Specialties that have underglazed decals.

Owning exclusive rights to the mold from which the signs are made, China Specialties is the only dealer that will ever sell these signs. Their enduring popularity with collectors make them an essential element in the China Specialties line.

1996 persimmon sign, $65; 1997 turquoise sign, $45; 1998-1999 chartreuse sign, $20; 1999 rose sign, $20; "Sunporch" sign, $25; "Mexicana" sign, $75. (Not shown) black "Moon Over Miami" sign, $25; periwinkle marked "turquoise" sign, $25.

Nursery Rhymes

Another example of the imaginative products developed by China Specialties are the Nursery Rhymes disk mini pitchers. Introduced in 1999, each pitcher is decorated with a vintage 1950s decal. There are six pitchers in the series including: Tom, Tom, the Piper's Son; Rub-a-dub, dub, Three Men in a Tub; Humpty Dumpty; Mary, Mary Quite Contrary; Ride a Cock Horse; and Old Mother Hubbard. The nursery rhymes are printed on the back of each pitcher. The bottom of each pitcher is marked, "A China Specialties Exclusive, Old Mother Goose Nursery Rhymes Series. Ltd. Edition of 500 per Rhyme."

"Nursery Rhymes" tumblers, $15.

Tom, Tom,
the Piper's Son
Stole a pig,
and away did run!
The Pig was eat,
And Tom was beat,
And Tom went crying
down the street.

Rub-a-dub, dub,
Three men in a tub,
And who do you
think they be?
The butcher, the baker,
The candlestick maker,
Turn them out, turn them out,
They are knaves all three!

Humpty Dumpty
Sat on a wall,
Humpty Dumpty
Had a great fall.
All the King's horses
and all the King's men,
Couldn't put Humpty
Together again.

Mary, Mary,
Quite contrary,
How does your garden grow?
With silver bells and
Cockle shells,
And pretty maids
All in a row.

Ride a
Cock Horse
to Banbury Cross,
To see a fine lady
upon a white horse.
With rings on her fingers
and bells on her toes,
She shall have music
Wherever she goes!

Old
Mother Hubbard
Went to the cupboard
To fetch her poor dog a bone;
But when she got there,
the cupboard was bare,
And so the poor dog
had none!

The nursery rhymes that appear on the back of "Nursery Rhymes" items.

Spoon Rest and Utensils—The Second Time Around

In 1997, China Specialties introduced a new version of an old spoon rest. Made by Hall China, and based on HLC's Rhythm spoon rest, the China Specialties spoon rest quickly became popular with many collectors. The Rhythm line was designed in 1950 by Don Schreckengost for F.W. Woolworth. Later in 1955 or early 1956 (HLC records don't give definitive dates), the spoon rest made its debut as a Harlequin item (apparently because of the similarity in colors between the two lines). While the vintage spoon rests were made in Rhythm/Harlequin yellow, forest green, and turquoise, and some were decorated with the American Provincial and Rhythm Rose decal, the new decal spoon rests were only made in white and ivory. The white spoon rests were decorated with Sunporch and Mexicana decals. The ivory spoon rests were produced with five different decals including: Orange Poppy, Red Poppy, Crocus, Silhouette, and the popular Hall Autumn Leaf design. While the new spoon rest may look like the vintage item, it's not really difficult to tell them apart. Of course, color and the decals are the first key to telling the new item from its vintage counterpart. Also, the handle on the new spoon rest is a little narrower at the top than the original spoon rest. The new spoon rest also has three points on the bottom that aren't glazed. Those areas are covered with three small tabs. All of the new spoon rests are clearly marked, indicating they are items made for China Specialties.

Their ceramic utensils comprise another of the China Specialties items based on a vintage HLC design. Released in 2001, they are made in Asia. Each item (the spoon, fork, and spatula) closely resembles the vintage Kitchen Kraft items that were produced in the 1930s. Manufactured in lilac, turquoise, and ivory, each color is almost a perfect match to the post 86 lilac and the vintage HLC turquoise and ivory colors. Because each item so closely resembles vintage HLC wares, the back of each item is clearly marked "CS" to prevent any confusion in the secondary marketplace.

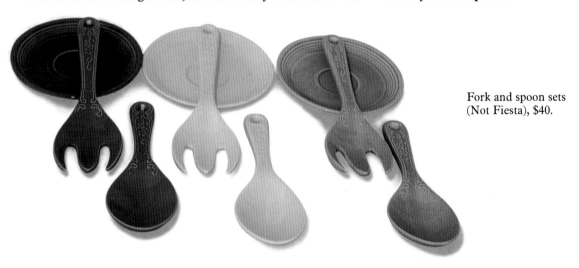

Fork and spoon sets (Not Fiesta), $40.

Mexicana

In 2000, China Specialties again introduced a line of products reminiscent of another vintage creation made by HLC — Mexicana. Like the Sunporch decals, the decals for the new line have been modified to appeal to today's collector. All the food contact surfaces are glazed in cobalt blue and all cups have undercoated lip rings. This new design does away with the need for Proposition 65 warning labels and makes the items safe to use as tableware. Unlike the Sunporch line, the Mexicana decals are varied. Several different types of decals are used in this line, adding variety to its design element. The same items offered in the Sunporch line were also offered in the new Mexicana line. These new items can be purchased at the East Liverpool Antique Mall.

"Mexicana" salt and pepper shakers, $33.

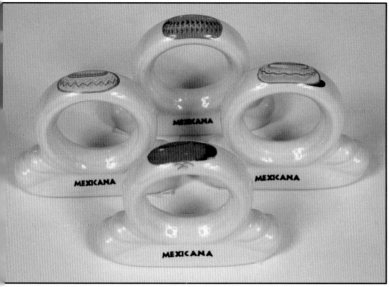

"Mexicana" napkin rings, $15 each.

"Mexicana" presentation bowl, $50.

"Mexicana" sauceboat, $30; carafe, $50; mug, $18.

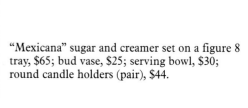

"Mexicana" 10 inch vase, $90; bud vase, $25.

"Mexicana" sugar and creamer set on a figure 8 tray, $65; bud vase, $25; serving bowl, $30; round candle holders (pair), $44.

"Mexicana" 2 cup teapot, $50; large teapot, $65; Seville ramekin condiment server, $50.

"Mexicana" spoon rest (made by Hall China), $40.

"Mexicana" large disk pitcher, $50; tumbler, $10.

"Mexicana" round handled serving tray, $33.

"Mexicana" butter dish, $30.

Other Items Made by China Specialties

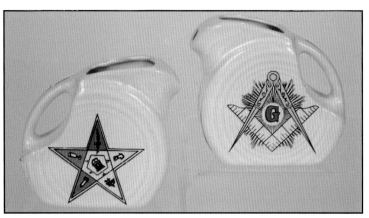

Masonic mini disk pitcher, $20.

1993 calendar plate in periwinkle blue, $50.

Christmas mini disk pitcher, $20.

Front and back view of the millennium bowl. The English collage artist, Hannah Dipper, designed the decal. $300-400.

Chapter 9

HLC Children's Ware and My First Fiesta

Fiesta Enters the Children's Market

HLC has produced several lines of children's chinaware. And with its happy, festive colors, it seems a natural that HLC would produce post 86 Fiesta for children. After all, kids need chinaware too. HLC is not alone, other makers of fine tableware such as Royal Doulton and Wedgwood are appealing to this growing market. Royal Doulton produces their "Classic Pooh" pattern that features a china plate, bowl, and cup decorated with Winnie the Pooh decals. Wedgwood produces " Peter Rabbit" children's dinnerware which offers a basic set of a mug, bowl, and plate. HLC saw an opportunity to establish a niche in the children's marketplace by offering cute, lovable dinner sets for children that were more affordable than either Wedgwood or Royal Doulton sets.

Jonathan believed the Fiesta line was a perfect choice for children's ware, not only because of its durability but also, and perhaps more importantly, because of it's sentimental value. Jonathan felt that many baby boomers, having grown up with Fiesta in their homes, would remember the part the dinnerware played in their family get-togethers and other special occasions around the dinner table. By offering parents and grandparents the opportunity to buy an affordable children's dinnerware touched by such heartfelt tradition, Jonathan believed that a line of Fiesta children's dinnerware would be a great success. He also said that by providing children with their own dinnerware, they too would remember the Fiesta plates of their childhood and, as adults, buy grown up Fiesta for their own homes.

HLC's first offering was the "Some Bunny's Been Eating Out of My Fiesta" children's set. Initially, this set was going to include a decaled coffee cup. Instead, a tumbler was substituted. Jonathan thought a cup might be difficult for very young children to use. Later on, however, a cup was introduced with other items in the set. Since this initial introduction, other children's patterns have been introduced. Sets with Christmas themes have included "Cookies for Santa" and "Tis the Season." "Baby's First Fiesta" is very popular with new moms and includes a bowl, a two handled cup, and a plate. This set, along with "The Noah's Ark Set," are Betty Crocker exclusives.

"Some Bunny's Been Eating Out of My Fiesta" on display at the 2000 International Housewares Show in Chicago, Illinois. CRV.

"Cookies For Santa." CRV.

My First Fiesta

What's your favorite childhood memory? For many grown up little girls (and, yes, little boys too), tea parties are very special treasured memories. "My First Fiesta" brings back these memories of simple pleasures and innocent times. Introduced in 1998 and initially sold through Bloomingdale's, it became one of HLC's top sellers.

Jonathan originally designed the child's tea set in 1996. And although the set didn't go into production at that time, the child's teapot did and was sold as the Fiesta two cup teapot. A few years later, during a visit to the HLC plant by several representatives of Bloomingdale's, Jonathan showed them samples from the children's tea set. They liked the idea and became very interested in the project.

The final teacup design came from the standard A.D. cup. Believing the stick handle made the cup harder for a child to hold, HLC used an AD handle from their restaurant line. The sugar bowl and creamer are designed to resemble their standard Fiesta counterparts, but were scaled down to fit a child's smaller hand. The eleven piece set is made up of a yellow teapot and lid, a rose cup and a periwinkle cup with matching saucers, two 6 inch yellow plates, a turquoise creamer, and a turquoise sugar bowl with matching lid. The set is very durable and is dishwasher safe. Additional cups and saucers for the set are offered in a variety of colors through Mega China. In addition to the original set, a Fiesta Dancing Lady set was also made; however, the Dancing Lady sets were not as popular as the original.

Another element of the tea set that appeals to customers is the artwork on the box. This is the work of Judi Noble (who succeeded Jonathan as art director at HLC). Instead of using a photograph, Judi wanted to design a label herself. Jonathan rejected her first rough draft of a Grandma with wire-rimmed glasses and gray hair pulled up in a bun, sitting at a little table with her granddaughter having a tea party, because he felt that the Grandma looked too old fashioned.

Jonathan told Judi that Grandmas—and even Great Grandmas—don't look like that today. Judi went back to work and created the box label we see today. Judi told me that the picture she created for the label was inspired by her own childhood memories.

As sweet as this set is, I'm sure it will sugar coat the childhood memories of many generations to come.

"Baby's First Fiesta" and "Noah's Ark" children's dinnerware.

"My First Fiesta" tea set decorated with a 2001 Fiesta Dancing Lady decal. *Photo courtesy of Ellie Rovella.* CRV.

"My First Fiesta" tea set. Box illustration by Judi Noble. *From the collection of Harvey Linn.* CRV.

Chapter 10

The Raspberry Bowl

In November 1997, HLC produced its 500 millionth piece of Fiesta. To commemorate the event, 500 individually numbered Raspberry Bowls were made. Fifteen of these bowls were donated to various charities, and the remaining bowls were distributed among the shareholders of HLC and members of the Aaron and Wells families. The Raspberry Bowl is the Holy Grail of any post 86 collection. Beautiful, sleek, stunning — all these adjectives still fall short of describing this most treasured piece of Fiesta.

During the initial phase of its creation, the art department discussed possible colors for the bowl and ways of making a glaze that would be difficult and too expensive to replicate. Other colors examined in place of the raspberry glaze included emerald green, red, and a very dark sapphire blue. The darker raspberry hue was chosen over lighter variations because, as a display piece, the darker hue would better complement the cabinets in which they were to be displayed. The pigment for the raspberry glaze comes from Europe. Some industry experts have suggested that the glaze is made from selenium, an expensive glaze pigment that is not made in the United States because of environmental regulations and is frequently imported from Europe. In its crystalline state, selenium is a dark red, and although elemental selenium is relatively non-toxic and is considered an essential trace element, hydrogen selenide and other selenium compounds are extremely toxic and resemble arsenic in their physiological reactions. Similar in color to cinnabar, raspberry is less red and has more of a burgundy hue.

Rumors have swirled within collector circles for years of the existence of test pieces made from the raspberry glaze. Such pieces do exist. Just like any other new glaze, test pieces were fired to make sure there would be no surprises when the Raspberry Bowls were fired. When test pieces came up missing, HLC management called the authorities and reported them stolen. Items rumored to exist include raspberry glazed pyramid candle holders, salt and pepper shakers, and lidded casserole dishes.

Sometimes referred to as the "Holy Grail" by Fiesta collectors, the raspberry bowl is stunning. *From the collection of Harvey Linn.*

According to Jonathan's son, Parker, Jonathan made this raspberry bowl for himself. Raspberry bowls made for HLC management, family members, and sold at charity auctions were numbered. *From the collection of Jonathan Parry.*

Chapter 11

The Fiesta 2000 Story

Jonathan was forever playing with thoughts and ideas about new designs and innovations. One of his ideas was that Fiesta was reaching a plateau insofar as sales and consumer interest. Jonathan wanted to take HLC into a new realm of dinnerware that would not just keep the company's momentum moving forward, but boost Fiesta sales as well. In one of our conversations, he told me that he first began to formulate the concept of what would become the Fiesta 2000 line as early as 1995. After giving much thought to these initial ideas, he finally approached HLC management to present his ideas and in 1998 began work in earnest on designing and producing the Fiesta 2000 line.

Initially, Jonathan and HLC produced four items from the Fiesta 2000 line: the 10 1/2 inch dinner plate, 14 1/2 inch charger, 9 inch deep plate, and a 7 1/2 inch luncheon plate. Showing them to prospective clients, the sales department used the items to get people's reaction to this fresh idea in dinnerware. HLC management liked the new line but some clients, like Bloomingdale's, were more cautious. It was new and it wasn't Fiesta.

It *was* new, a whole new idea in dinnerware. Jonathan described it as the first new thing in dinnerware that had come out in forty years. He envisioned it as a more casual line of dinnerware with each item in the line serving more than one function. For instance, a deep plate could double as a soup bowl and a dessert bowl could double as a saucer. Another innovation was how it was designed to be used with another completely different line of dinnerware, the Fiesta line. Each item in the Fiesta 2000 line was specially sized so that the two lines would fit inside each other. By using the Fiesta colors and by adding three small complementary curved lines around each plate well in the Fiesta 2000 items, Jonathan's new design tied the two dinnerware lines together. Jonathan hoped its highly stylized, contemporary motif, reminiscent of the 1950s, would appeal to consumers. Given the green light by HLC management, he started his design for a pitcher and, adding a mug to the line, prepared to showcase his new dinnerware on January 16, 2000, the opening day of the International Housewares Show in Chicago.

The pitcher design proved to be a challenge for the art department to produce. A complex piece, it took many tedious hours to model. On January 11, Jonathan became ill at work and was rushed to the hospital. His loyal staff, unable to work or concentrate, awaited word on his condition and the pitcher was not completed on time for the line's debut in Chicago. Standing in for Jonathan, Judi Noble went to Chicago with HLC's marketing director, Dave Conley, and introduced Fiesta 2000. Within the industry, the line received outstanding reviews. Articles in the *Chicago Tribune* and *USA Today* praised its styling and predicted its success in the marketplace. Still, major department stores were hesitant to commit to the new line. Cautiously, a few major chains decided to test the public's reaction by offering the new line in limited areas of the country. During his recovery, Jonathan returned to work, the pitcher was completed, and more pieces were added to the Fiesta 2000 line.

Fiesta 2000 received mixed reviews from consumers. Some didn't like the way it looked and others didn't like the name. Dave Conley queried various online Fiesta collector boards, asking for suggestions on what to call the new line. Suggestions poured in, running the gamut from "Metropolis" and "Deco" to "What is That?" and "Conley Kraft." However, all these suggestions were put aside when Bloomingdale's and other chains insisted the name carry the word Fiesta. When asked what he wanted to call the line, Jonathan replied, "I don't care what people call it. I'm about the design and the concept, not the name."

Jonathan had hoped to create fifteen unique items. Unfortunately, he never completed the line. Initially, after his death, HLC eagerly promoted the new dinnerware, but in the end, it was discontinued. Without Jonathan at the helm developing his new product, the project started to unravel. Many HLC customers like Bloomingdale's, who had always trusted Jonathan's instincts about the marketplace, had misgivings about investing large amounts of capital in a new unconventional dinnerware line without Jonathan's leadership. Officially,

HLC cited the major department stores as the reason for the discontinuation of the line, saying the stores wanted the company to focus on Fiesta and increase the number of products available in the Fiesta line. However, there is some indication that technical difficulties may have precluded further development of any new Fiesta 2000 items.

Some HLC collectors believe that since the Fiesta 2000 was made for such a short period, items from the line will be highly sought after in years to come. The Fiesta 2000 items were made in cobalt blue, persimmon, and pearl gray. Twenty-four Fiesta 2000 pitchers, donated by HLC, were auctioned by the East Liverpool High School Alumni Association on June 17, 2001 to raise money for its scholarship fund. Someday Fiesta 2000 dinnerware indeed may be highly collectible, but at the time of this writing it is readily available. As HLC continues to make strides in the china industry, the Fiesta 2000 is now a part of its rich past.

The Fiesta 2000			
	Modeling Date	Model Number	Size
Dinner plate	12/7/98	H-5289	10 1/2"
Charger	12/21/98	H-5291-1	14 1/2"
Deep plate	1/11/99	H-5293	9"
Luncheon plate	1/25/99	H-5296	7 1/4"
Mug	8/30/99	H-5335	12 oz.
Saucer	11/10/99	H-5342	6 3/4"
Dessert	11/12/99	H-5345	6 3/4"
Cereal bowl	1/10/00	H-5354	Not available
Pitcher	Not available	Not available	10 1/4"
Salad plate	Not available	Not available	9"

Persimmon dinner and salad plate. Juniper fruit bowl and saucer. CRV.

This Fiesta 2000 pitcher in juniper is a very rare test piece. The pitcher was slated for general distribution until HLC discontinued further development of the line. *Photo by Mark Burnett. From the collection of Mark and Cathy Burnett.* NEV.

Cobalt blue Fiesta 2000 mug. *From the collection of Harvey Linn.* CRV.

Chapter 12

Fiesta—American Icon

When Fiesta was introduced in 1936 during the great depression, it was an inexpensive tableware made to meet the needs of the everyday person; but more than seventy-five years later, Fiesta is now an American cultural icon. Once a favorite pastime for a small niche of pottery collectors that didn't have a lot of money to spend, Fiesta is now collected by the rich and famous and commands high prices in the secondary market. When pop artist Andy Warhol passed away and his Fiesta collection went on the auction block, collectors lined up and paid thousands of dollars to have a bit of Warhol history in their Fiesta collection. Even household diva, Martha Stewart, finds Fiesta "inspiring." Noted author Jeffrey B. Snyder has been a guest on Martha's popular television show several times to talk about the colorful dinnerware and collectors have spotted pieces of Fiesta on the set of her television show.

Much of the public's renewed interest in Fiesta is due, in part, to its reintroduction into the marketplace in 1986; but, another reason relates to advancements made in mass communication technology, most notably, the internet. Thousands of web sites sell Fiesta and, since the advent of the internet, collectors can now communicate with each other about their common interest on collector boards and via e-mail. With a click of a mouse, those hard-to-find pieces collectors used to spend years looking for can now be found on auction web pages like e-Bay or online with the help of other collectors that sign on daily to collector web boards. Internet collector communities developed and, with them, new clubs and organizations. The Homer Laughlin China Collectors Association (HLCCA) was formed in 1998. Members communicate online and friendships are formed between people that sometimes never meet face to face; but, once a year many members of the organization do meet at the annual HLCCA convention. During the conventions collectors buy, sell, and trade vintage and post 86 Fiesta and also exhibit their collections. Awards are given to the participants with the best displays. The HLCCA quarterly magazine, *The Dish*, is written by collectors for collectors. Each edition is filled with valuable information about Fiesta and other Homer Laughlin China lines.

The community around Newell, West Virginia, the home of the Homer Laughlin China Company, has also benefited from the popularity of Fiesta. Tourism is now an important element in the small community's economy. Tourists from around the country converge on Newell and the nearby town of East Liverpool, Ohio, to buy Fiesta in local antique malls and to attend a yearly pottery auction and festival. The East Liverpool High School Alumni Association (ELHSAA) has raised thousands of dollars for its college scholarship fund by auctioning off pottery donated by local pottery companies. The Homer Laughlin China Company enthusiastically supports the auctions and donates unique, limited numbered Fiesta items to the auction every year. Many of the items donated by HLC have sold for several thousand dollars. The popularity of Fiesta among collectors has helped promote an improved quality of life for the community's youth.

Another important tourist attraction is the Homer Laughlin China Company factory and its outlet store. The outlet store's semi-annual outlet sale attracts Fiesta vendors and collectors from all over the country and the crowds keep growing every year. During the sale, people sleep in front of the outlet in lawn chairs and sleeping bags waiting for the doors to open. HLC supports local community groups by allowing them to sell food and drinks to the crowds waiting in long lines to get into the outlet. Pat Shreve, the manager at the outlet store, said that some of her customers plan their vacations around the outlet sale. One woman I spoke with said she came to the outlet store sale from out of state because her daughter was getting married and instead of renting dishes for the wedding reception, she and her family decided to take a trip to Newell to buy their dishes. After the wedding she planed to distribute the dishes among her three daughters. The woman said she wanted her daughters to have a remembrance of the wedding and to have dishes for their new homes when they got married. The outlet store is also home to the HLC museum. The museum is typically open to the public after a factory tour. If you are a fan of any type of HLC pottery, it's something you shouldn't miss.

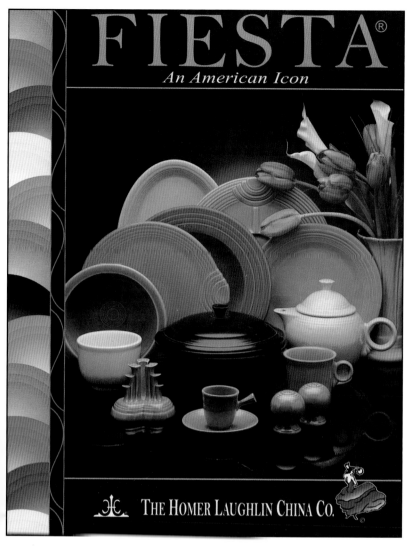

FIESTA®
An American Icon

THE HOMER LAUGHLIN CHINA CO.®

Brochure courtesy of the Homer Laughlin China Company.

The Fine Art of
Philip J. Carroll

Fiesta has found its way into modern art. Philip J. Carroll's art can be found in many prestigious collections including McGraw Hill Companies Permanent Collection in New York City, New York. This picture is entitled "Five Fiesta." Oil on Canvas, 40 inches x 50 inches, collection of the artist.

Many collectors use Fiesta ephemera to decorate their home. My friend framed this ad and proudly displays it in his living room. *Photos courtesy of Rick Benning.*

Some collectors like to mix their post 86 Fiesta with other vintage HLC lines. White post 86 Fiesta is pictured with Sky Tone dinnerware. *Photo courtesy of Patrick Masterson.*

The next generation of Fiesta collectors having a tea party using a set of "My First Fiesta."

Post 86 Fiesta is seen everywhere including television shows and newspaper and magazine ads. This picture is of current Boston Market ad picturing a post 86 Fiesta platter.

There are many internet sites devoted to Fiesta dinnerware and other HLC dinnerware lines. One of my favorite sites is GOFIESTA.com. *Photo courtesy of Fred Mutchler.*

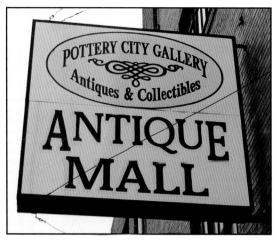

Pottery City Gallery Antiques and Collectibles is a great place to shop. It is located in East Liverpool, Ohio, just across the river from Newell, West Virginia, the home of HLC.

A sign that welcomes travelers to Newell, West Virginia.

A sign in East Liverpool, Ohio, advertising the annual pottery auction benefiting the ELHSAA (East Liverpool High School Alumni Association).

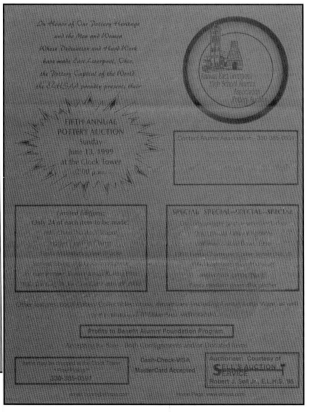

Flyers advertising the pottery auction. *Flyers courtesy of Gary Schroiner.*

A crystalline carafe and vase made for the 2001 ELHSAA pottery auction. HLC opted not to produce crystalline items because the glaze is too impractical for mass production. *From the collection of Jeryl and Gary Schreiner.* Vase and carafe, $1,000-1,200.

Some people just can't get enough of a good thing. Examples of the black millennium I vase, the juniper millennium III vase, and the chartreuse coffeepot. *Photo courtesy of Gary Schreiner.*

The HLC store sign leading to the HLC factory outlet store.

A souvenir cup from the outlet store sale featuring Judi Noble's character, Ms. Bea. CRV.

There are long lines of people waiting to enter and check out of the store during the outlet store sale.

From Russia, With Love

Troy Williams is a young man with a great sense of humor who has a friend that loves post 86 Fiesta. To make his friend, Doug Warzyn, feel more at home when he visits Troy for dinner, Troy bought a set of post 86 Fiesta in persimmon so his friend wouldn't have to eat from an "inferior" plate. When Troy found out he was going to Russia on a research trip, he took one of Doug's plates with him and photographed it in front of many famous places. Now when Doug comes to visit, he eats from one of the most traveled post 86 Fiesta plates known to exist. Troy posted this picture on his web page. The picture shows Troy holding a plate in front of the Historical Museum just off Red Square in Moscow.

Troy Williams holding the most traveled piece of post 86 Fiesta in the world. *Photo courtesy of Troy Williams.*

Afterword

History has a way of repeating itself and home fashion trends are no exception. When Fiesta was first introduced in 1936, it set the trend of an entire industry; but, by the 1950s its popularity started to fade. Although the colors were updated and part of the line was restyled, it never regained its momentum in the marketplace and the line was finally laid to rest in 1972. Perhaps history is now repeating itself in the retail market, as the popularity of post 86 seems to be fading. It is still a strong contender for the retail consumer's dollar but as its popularity wanes, retailers are carrying fewer colors and the display space in their stores is getting smaller and less prominent. The colors are now being updated, as evidenced by the introduction of plum and the phasing out of gray and rose. Coincidentally, these were two of the 1950s colors that were phased out when HLC tried to update Fiesta's look once before. After Frederick Rhead's death, there were no new designs added to the line. Instead, HLC, under the leadership of their talented art director, Don Schreckengost, concentrated on new dinnerware lines. Since Jonathan's death, HLC has tried to introduce some decal items to the post 86 line with, at best, lukewarm results and there are no new lines of dinnerware being designed with home-use in mind. If history continues to repeat itself and no new innovative designs are introduced, post 86 Fiesta, like the vintage Fiesta, will be discontinued in the retail market.

Jonathan once told me that he didn't understand why collectors were so crazy about Fiesta, "...after all, they're just dishes." Since his passing I have donated several pictures of some of the prototypes Jonathan had given me to the Smithsonian Museum. The Smithsonian collects objects that define life in America.

Yes, Jonathan, they are just dishes — and a whole lot more.

Where to Buy Fiestaware

More of my favorite places to buy Fiestaware. Many other resources are available on the web.

Fiesta Collector at www.fiestacollector.com
Homer Laughlin China Company at www.hlchina.com
Mega China at www.megachina.com
Phiesta's Fiesta at www.phiesta.com
Fiesta Plus at www.fiestaplus.com
Tomorrow's Vintage: 22dino@msn.com
Macy's at www.macys.com
Bloomingdale's at www.bloomingdales.com
Betty Crocker at www.bettycrocker.com
J.C. Penney's at www.penneys.com

Table Top Direct
740 Marks Road
Valley City, OH 44280
Phone 330-225-3684
Fax 330273-8267

Hot Plates
New Hope, PA
1-888-869-3220

Explore the web and check out these informative Fiesta web sites.

Medium Green at wwwmediumgreen.com
GOFIESTA at www.GOFIESTA.com
Circa 36 at www.pcis.net/geocat
Fiesta Fanatic at www.fiestafanatic.com
Ohio River Pottery at wwwOhioRiverPottery.com (an superb site for information on a wide variety of pottery).
Post Modern Fiesta at www.geocities.com/SoHo/café/1953/fiesta/fiesta.htm
Steve Beals Home Page: HLC Tour - Resources and Links (excellent online tour of the HLC factory) at www.members.aol.com/hlfiesta/tour/resource.htm

For information about the HLCCA, log on to their web site at www.HLCCA.com.
For further information about the artwork of Philip Carroll, visit his homepage at www.philipjcarroll. com.

China Specialties
PO Box 361280
Strongsvillie, Ohio 44136-1280

156

Suggested Values

Suggested values listed in the book are for items in mint condition. Items in mint condition are glazed evenly and are free of scratches, chips, and glaze skips. In addition, decals on items must be intact and free of any visual damage. Items with light scratching are generally worth 30% below book price. Items with heavy scratching or that are chipped in any way are worth 50%-60% below book value. When buying lids and bases separately, the general rule is lids make up 60% of the value of an item while the base makes up the remaining 40%.

The suggested values in this book are meant only to be used as a guide. Prices for items will vary from one regional area to another and items found in antique malls for premium prices can sometimes be found on e-Bay for below book price. Values can also fluctuate widely depending on announcements from HLC. When HLC announced that pyramid candle holders were being discontinued, prices climbed and when they reversed their decision, the values came back down. Values for this book were determined by a survey of Fiesta dealers and collectors and an averaging of e-Bay prices over a period of six months.

Two pricing codes will be used throughout the book. They are NEV: no established value and CRV: current retail value.

(Table 1) Price Guide

	Lilac	Sapphire
Bouillon cup 6 3/4 oz.	$35-40	NP
Bowl, small 14 oz.	$25-35	NP
Bowl, rim pasta 12"	$60-90	NP
Bowl, rim soup 9"	$45-60	NP
Bowl, serving 39 1/4 oz.	$45-60	$30-45
Bowl, medium 19 oz.	$30-40	$15-20
Bowl, stacking cereal 6 1/2"	$30-45	NP
Bowl, stacking fruit 5 3/8"	$30-40	NP
Butter dish, cover	$60-75	NP
Candle holder, pyramid (tripod)	$500-600 (pair)	NEV
Candle holder, round (bulb)	$100-130 (pair)	NEV
Carafe	NEV	$35-45
Casserole	$160-230	NP
Coffee server, covered	$160-235	NEV

	Lilac	Sapphire
Creamer 7 oz. (standard)	$35-45	NEV
Cup, A.D. with saucer	$100-145	NP
Cup, tea	$20-35	$10-15
Mug, Fiesta (Tom and Jerry)	$25-40	NEV
Napkin ring	$75-100	NEV
Pie baker, 10 1/4"	$75-100	NP
Pitcher, disk juice	$60-95	NEV
Pitcher, disk mini	$40-60	NEV
Pitcher, disk large	$60-80	$40-50
Plate, dinner 10 1/2"	$35-45	$25-35
Plate, luncheon 9"	$35-45	NP
Plate, salad 7 1/4"	$25-35	NP
Plate, bread & butter 6 1/8"	$15-20	$20-25
Plate, chop 11 3/4"	$50-75	NP
Platter, oval 9 5/8"	$40-50	NP
Platter, oval 11 5/8"	$40-50	NP
Platter, oval 13 5/8"	$40-50	$30-40
Sauceboat	$50-60	NEV
Saucer, tea	$10-15	$10-15
Salt and pepper shakers	$45-60 (pair)	NEV
Sugar bowl, covered (standard)	$35-45	NEV
Sugar & Creamer on Figure 8 Tray	$70-90	NEV (no tray)
Teapot, 44 oz. covered	$75-125	NEV
Tray, relish (corn on the cob)	$35-50	NP
Tray, round tab handle	NEV	$50-70
Tray, hostess 12"	NEV	NP
Tumbler	$20-30	$15-20
Vase, bud	$80-110	NEV
Vase, medium	$300-350	$250-300

(Table 2) Fiesta Mates

	Lilac	Sapphire
Jumbo cup 18 oz.	$30-45	$25-35
Jumbo saucer	$15-25	$10-15
Jumbo bowl (chili bowl)	$20-30	NP
Sugar caddy	$50-75	NP
Colonial teapot	NEV	NP

NEV: No established value. Many lilac and sapphire pieces that were not massed produced and released to the general public are known to exist in private collections. Because of the rarity of many of these items, and because many have not been sold in the secondary market, it is difficult to establish their value. Other sapphire and lilac items may exist.

NP: Not produced.

(Table 3) Specialty Items

The following tables are suggested values for specialty items not shown in the book.

Fiesta Club of America

1996 persimmon tab handle server $25-45
1998 chartreuse tab handle server $25-45
1998 black tab handle server $25-45
1999 pearl gray tab handle server $25-45

(Table 4) 60th Anniversary Disk Pitcher Sets

Turquoise $45-50	Persimmon $45-50
Rose $325-375	Periwinkle blue $45-50 Cobalt blue
$50-60	

(Table 5) Moon Over Miami (Black)

Sauceboat $90	Serving bowl $30
Mini disk pitcher $26	Covered casserole $120
Coffee Pot $120	Tumbler $15
Tripod candle holder $60	Seville ramkin $10
A.D. cup and saucer $30	A.D. cup and saucer $30
Mug $18	Covered butter dish $30
Clock $200-250	

Moon Over Miami (Noon Over Miami on turquoise)

Carafe $45	Mug $15
Medium vase $70	3 leg salsa bowl $25
Napkin ring $10	Sauceboat $35
Handled serving tray $50	Sugar packet holder $20
Demi cup and saucer $25	Mini disk pitcher $30
Juice disk pitcher $35	Serving bowl $28
Small salt and pepper shakers $30	Range top salt and pepper shakers $40
Sugar and creamer on figure 8 tray $60	

Sunporch and Mexicana (Use same value list for all Mexicana and Sunporch items)

Individual sugar bowl $30	Individual creamer $22 Sugar
packet holder $18	Coffee server $50
Clock (Sunporch only) $150	Juice disk pitcher $33
Mini disk pitcher $35	Relish tray $35
Jumbo mug $15	Range top salt & pepper
shakers $45	

(Table 6) WB Fiesta

Tweety "Dewicious!" Series

9" rim soup bowl $15-25	Casserole $35-40
Range top S&P shakers $45-60	9" dinner plate $22-27
Teacup and saucer $20-25	9" serving bowl $25-30

Bugs Bunny "What's Cookin, Doc?" Series

9" dinner plate $22-27

Daffy Duck "It's Mine, All Mine" Series

9" dinner plate $22-27
12" tab handled serving tray $45-55

Sylvester "Sufferin' Succotash" Series

9" dinner plate $22-27	10" pie baker $35-45

Porky Pig "That's All Folks!" Series

9" dinner plate $22-27	Coffee mug $10-15
8 1/4" serving bowl $80-125	Teacup and saucer $20-25
9" rim soup bowl $15-25	

Scooby-Doo "Scooby Snack" Series (on white and sea mist green)

9" rim soup bowl $15-20
Teacup and saucer $20-25
Looney Times Fiesta Clock $50-75

Select Bibliography & References

Books

Conroy, Barbara J. *Restaurant China: Volume 1*. Paducah, KY: Collector Books, 1998.

_____. *Restaurant China: Volume 2*. Paducah: Collector Books, 1999.

Cunningham, Jo. *Homer Laughlin, A Giant Among Dishes: 1873-1939*. Atglen, PA: Schiffer Publishing Ltd., 1998.

_____. *Homer Laughlin China: 1940s & 1950s*. Atglen: Schiffer Publishing Ltd., 2000.

Gonzalez, Mark. *Collecting Fiesta, Lu-Ray & Other Colorware*. Gas City, IN: L-W Book Sales, 2000.

Homer Laughlin China Collectors Association. *Fiesta, Harlequin, & Kitchen Kraft Dinnerwares*. Atglen, PA: Schiffer Publishing Ltd., 2000.

Huxford, Sharon and Bob. *The Collector's Encyclopedia of Fiesta*. 6th ed. Paducah, KY: Collector Books, 1987.

_____. *The Collector's Encyclopedia of Fiesta*. 8th ed. Paducah, KY: Collector Books, 1998.

_____. *The Collector's Encyclopedia of Fiesta*. 9th ed. Paducah, KY: Collector Books, 2001.

Kay, Ronald E., Taylor, Kathleen M., Kay, Sara M. *1999 FCoA Fiesta Price Guide, Book 3*. Love's Park: Fiesta Club of America, Inc., 1999.

Snyder, Jeffrey B. *Fiesta: Homer Laughlin China Company's Colorful Dinnerware*. 3rd ed. Atglen, PA: Schiffer Publishing Ltd., 2000.

Articles

Amblin, Kathleen. "Looney for Fiesta," *The Dish*, vol.1, no. 3 (1999): 7, 13.

American Ceramic Society Bulletin, "Homer Laughlin China: Strong Commitment to the Future," vol. 73, no. 9 (September 1994): 65-67.

Daly, Ann. "A man and his Jewelry," *Pittsburgh Press*, (Thursday, February 10, 1983): B-7.

Fagerlin, Candy. "Dish Tales With Jonathan Parry ... The Interview!," *The Dish*, vol. 2, no. 1 (1999): 8-12.

Fagerlin, Candy. "Milly Fever," *The Dish*, vol. 2, no. 2 (1999-2000): 8-9.

"Looney Tunes Homer Laughlin Fiestaware," http://www.geocities.com/televisioncity/set/8681/fiesta.html.

"Pennsylvania Weddings," http://www.paweddings.com/fiesta.htm.

Polick, Terri. "Pick Your Color," *The Dish*, vol. 2, no. 2 (1999-2000): 12-13,15.

_____. "My First Fiesta," *The Dish*, vol. 2, no. 3 (2000): 4.

_____. "The HLC Outlet Store Sale," *The Dish*, vol. 2, no. 4 (summer 2000): 4-5.

_____. "Aloha Homer!," *The Dish*, vol. 2, no. 4 (summer 2000): 8-9.

_____. "The Second Time Around," *The Dish*, vol. 3, no. 1 (fall 2000): 10.

Prop 65 News, "Proposition 65 Made Simple," http://prop65news.com/pubs/brochure/madesimple.html.

Sample, Ann. "Homer Laughlin Continues To Expand Fiesta Franchise," *HFN: The Weekly Newspaper for the Home Furnishing Network*, (May 10, 1999): 34.

Sheridan, Patricia. "Fiesta Ware fans out," (Pittsburgh) *post-gazette.com Magazine*, (Wednesday, March 17, 1999).

Sheridan, Patricia. "Fiesta Ware licensing new line of products," (*Pittsburgh Post-Gazette*) *reporternews.com*, (Wednesday, April 21, 1999).

Society of Glass and Ceramic Decorators. "The Decorator's Difference," http://www.ceramics.com/sgcd/update399_2.html.

Walker, Liz. "The New Go-alongs...," *The Dish*, vol. 1, no. 4 (1999): 12,14-15.

Wilson, Joel. "For FCQ Members Only," *Fiesta Collector's Quarterly*, no.17 (winter 1995).

_____. "Lots of Rumors on Lilac," *Fiesta Collector's Quarterly*, no.20 (fall 1996).

_____. "New introduction in Moon Over Miami," *Fiesta Collector's Quarterly*, no.25 (winter 1997/98).

_____. "Item Available for Shipment to FCQ members," *Fiesta Collector's Quarterly*, no. 33 (winter 99/2000).

_____. "Some Items in Turquoise Moon Over Miami (Noon Over Miami)," *Fiesta Collector's Quarterly*, no.35 (summer 2000).

_____. "Farewell to Fiestaware 2000," *Fiesta Collector's Quarterly*, no.36 (fall 2000).

_____. "Cinnabar Is The Newest Color," *Fiesta Collector's Quarterly*, no.37 (winter 2000/01).

Index